SONG TITLE SERIES

AC/DC

JOAN MAGUIRE

Copyright Page

New: AC/DC

Author: Joan Maguire

National Library of Australia Cataloguing-in-Publication – Public entry

Author:	Maguire, Joan
Title:	AC / DC / Joan Maguire
ISBN	978-0-9808551-2-8
Series:	Song title series
Subjects:	AC/DC
	AC/DC (Musical group)
	Rock musicians—Australia—Biography
	Rock groups—Australia--Biography

Dewey Number: 781.66092

Published with the assistance of Love of Books and is available through the Print on Demand network andwww.songtitleseries.com

This book is also available in a large print formant and as an E-book.

This short story book was created and written
By Joan Maguire on 16th August 2010 ©
ISBN: 978-0-9808551-2-8

E-book re-written April 2014© and is available through the
providers listed on www.songtitleseries.com
EISBN: 978-0-9808551-9-7

The large print book is available through the same
distributors as the normal book and
www.songtitleseries.com
ISBN: 978-0-9941998-8-1 (large print)

DEDICATION

I would like to dedicate this book and say to thank you to my Earth Angel David and his friends, who inspire and motivate me to achieve things that I never dreamt, were possible.

And to Kylie, for without her this book would not have been written.

INTRODUCTION

I first got the idea for my books as I was watching one of the concerts that Bon Jovi did at Madison Square Garden in 2009, with a friend.

I wrote my first short story book using Bon Jovi song titles and as I like a challenge, I decided to try bigger stories using more song titles from different bands. There are so many bands and artists around that I decided to write this book for one of my daughters who is an avid AC/DC follower.

Legally I can not use Lyrics or Music because of Copyright but I can use song titles so a total of 916 song titles (Italicized) have been used to make this story possible. Also due to the nature of my books; legally I must place a Reference (exactly as it is down loaded) and Bibliography in the back of the book.

Come and join the tour group as they travel down the *Highway to Hell* from the beginning of the highway in Black Hills territory to the town of *Hells Bells* at the other end. A tour guide will explain about the different towns/cities such as *Sin City* and *Decibel* that you will pass through or bypass and suggests you visit some attractions along the way. *Hells Bells* is the place you want to visit because in the end, *Hell ain't a bad place to be*.

When reading this "Song Title Series" book, I hope that no disservice has been done to the band as well as their adoring fans who read it, for that was not my intention. As I may have missed a song, an album or a concert within this book I do apologize sincerely. I have created and written this story without the sanctity of the band and I hope that if they read this they will enjoy it as well.

It's now time to sit back with a drink and enjoy reading this story and don't forget that because of using the original song titles in whole, there are places in the book that I could not change to make it more comprehensible for you the reader.

ACKNOWLEDGEMENTS

I would like to thank my daughters, Jenny and Kylie for their positive but critical input in the first draft of this book. With taking their input to mind, I have improved and slightly changed this book.

I would also like to thank my son Peter and his family for their support and help in keeping me grounded.

I would like to thank Kay and Julie for their patience and understanding whilst teaching me and giving me the skills to present my unique books in the best way possible.

I would also like to thank everyone else who has helped me bring this book to life and to you for buying it.

OTHER BOOKS IN THE SONG TITLE SERIES

CONTENTS

BEGINNINGS

"Welcome, welcome everybody to the last leg of your Mystery Tours. You have been on three different tours that have combined here today. My name is Jo and I will be your guide for the rest of your trip.

I have been asked "Where does the *Highway to Hell* start, where does it finish, and what's in between the two?"

Well, let's climb aboard the bus and take a trip and I will explain to you as we go. *Now are you ready?"* said Jo.

"The *Highway to Hell* starts as a dirt track somewhere up high and way *back in Black* Hills country. On its way south it changes into a highway and the first place it passes through is *SIN CITY* that could be classed as a mining town, although a lot more has happened there besides mining but *dirty deeds done dirt cheap* was not available in this town. We will stop there for about an hour for lunch.

In the mining side of employment, the ground is as *hard as a rock;* therefore a lot of *T.N.T.* is used in breaking it up. The blasts would *shake your foundations* to the point where at night the townsfolk thought their houses would collapse, and in the mornings, they would tell the work crews *"You shook me all night long* again."

The mining crews, known as the Rough Nuts, use two machines one called *The Jack,* and one called a *Whole Lotta Rosie* which is named after Rosie, a big black Southern woman who grew up where the dirt track starts in the Black Hills with her six older brothers. She is not only feared in these parts, but well respected as well and lives in the town.

Whole Lotta Rosie, the machine, is like a big *Ballbreaker* and the Rough Nuts using her would often say, because of the different soils underground, *"Let there be rock, let there be rock* and lots of it," just so they could fit the *big ball* to *Whole Lotta Rosie* and with a *flick of the switch* they would pound the rock until it became a pile of rubble. The Rough Nuts would shout as they worked "Ha! *Got you by the balls."*

The Jack, another type of equipment, would also *shake your foundations. The Jack* drills a hole into the rock or into the ground where *T.N.T.* would be placed deep in the hole. Then with the *flick of the switch,* the *live wire* would send a *high voltage* current to the *T.N.T.* that would create a huge explosion.

2

Again because of the soil type the Rough Nuts would often say *"Let there be rock,* please *let there be rock."* because they liked using *The Jack* even though there was a danger of it causing a *landslide.*

Hells bells if you were too slow to *shake a leg* and get out of there before the explosion, because you could end up either having a *nervous shakedown* or getting *shot down in flames* as the guys called the red dust that was omitted by the explosion.

They all said *"Let there be rock,"* because they didn't know really what was deep beneath the soil and if there was clay or sand then the machines wouldn't work as well as it should and the heavy duty vehicles would have to be brought in to finish the job.

The rock and dirt was then taken down the *Highway to Hell* to smelters on the other side of *Sin City.*

One morning some of the townies approached the miners and said *"You shook me all night long* with the explosions."

The Rough Nuts replied "It wasn't us because it rained last night and we can only use the *T.N.T* when it's dry. You must have been dreaming or heard thunder and thought it was us."

In the evenings, some of the townies would meet at the *House of Jazz* that Rosie owned to listen to the *Bad Boy Boogie* band. Some of the men say that Rosie ain't got a *stiff upper lip* 'cos *she's got balls.* There's no *beating around the bush* when dealing with her because if she thought that you were *riff raff* or dead drunk, she would say *"Let's make it* a night now, so go home and come back tomorrow." and you left because you never wanted Rosie to repeat herself.

The *House of Jazz* was an unusual place because they played any type of music from *Crabsody in Blue* to *Bad Boy Boogie* to rock and roll. This was a place where you could *rock your heart* out listening to the *rock 'n' roll singer,* or listen to some country music, or get yourself lost in the blues. An old *rocker* would tell you that *rock and roll ain't noise pollution;* in fact *rock 'n' roll damnation* was a way of life.

On their days off, the Rough Nuts would often be *back in black* jeans, long sleeved shirts and hiking boots and after *givin' the dog a bone* they would take a short *ride on* the train to the *Badlands* Rifle Range.

The range had *guns for hire* where you could *shoot to thrill* the observers when you either *sink the pink* ball that floated on a small pond or hit the bullseye that would send out a noise that sounded like you were being *thunderstruck*. *If you want blood* then this was not the place to get it.

Every now and then a *problem child* would grow up and visit the range. They would *shoot to thrill* themselves, knowing that they had the knowledge and the ability to injure or kill something but not someone.

If the misfit was caught misusing the *guns for hire* and had grown to working age, they were sent to work on *The Jack* at the mines. It was hoped that because of the *danger* involved in the using the equipment, it would teach the misfit to be responsible to when it came to using *guns for hire* or *T.N.T.* There had only been one *problem child* in the past two years and they learnt the lesson about being responsible when they nearly seriously injured themselves and their workmate.

Another reason for the decline of problem children or misfits was that about two years ago, a *jailbreak* happened in a neighboring county and a few of the escapees decided to hide out in some hidden caves situated up high and way *back in Black* Hills county.

A few local boys had *gone shootin'* for the day with the *guns for hire* and stumbled across the escapees and tried to capture them. There was a bit of *ruff stuff* going on before a local male yelled to the escapees *"If you want blood, you've got it*. It will be your blood as we will *not shoot to thrill* but we will shoot to kill.

We know that you are the men from the *jailbreak* and if you dare to try and run, you'll find that *it's a long way to the top* and we know every inch of these hills, so you won't get far. Make your choice, *give it up* or get shot?"

The escapees said "OK, don't *fire your guns,* we're coming out, besides jail is like hell and after living on *the razor's edge* and with all the trouble we've had so far whilst being on the run and fighting with you lot, *hell ain't a bad place to be* after all."

The boys tied the escapees together at the waist so they couldn't slip away back into the hills and marched them down the *Highway to Hell* to *Sin City* and handed them over to the authorities who took the escapees *back in black* vans to jail.

The news of the escapees being returned to confinement made the younger people realize what it was like living with freedom therefore curtailing their ideas of becoming a *problem child* or getting into serious trouble with the law.

We are now pulling into the town and will be parking beside the best café in town. Feel free to have a bit of a look around the town but remember we are only going to stay here for about an hour."

THE BEST THING

"Now that everyone is back on board we will continue to travel south, and the next town on the *Highway to Hell* is *CLASSIC ROCK*. A town where *dirty deeds done dirt cheap* are prolific and where *rock 'n' roll damnation* is a way of life. They say "That *money talks* in this town and that it's a *dog eat dog* world here."

If you want blood, you've got it because they don't *shoot to thrill* but shoot to kill. A *problem child* is a normal child and can be a *live wire* as well as being as *hard as a rock* with a *mean streak.*

We will be staying here for the night in a very well run, secure hotel in the safe side of town.

The town became this way many, many years ago, when six men who were amongst a group involved in a very elaborate *jailbreak* evaded re-capture. They first went to *Sin City* and found out what a *whole lotta Rosie* was all about. They found out that *she's got balls* and she would *walk all over you* if you were not careful.

If you looked like *riff raff* to her then she would not go *beating around the bush* in telling you so. It was made clear that *dirty deeds done dirt cheap* would not be tolerated in her town. *If you want blood* then you wouldn't get it there because the regulations for firearms were that *guns for hire* only was allowed which meant that no-one was allowed to own one and if you were caught abusing the firearm rules, then you would have to work in the mines with the *T.N.T.*

The escapees left *Sin City* after saying to a *whole lotta Rosie* "*You ain't got a hold on me* and you never will have." and disappeared back into the Black Hills where they hid for three months despite another thorough search of the area by the police. They then moved to Classic Rock where they took over the town.

Even though, as some of the citizens would say, "During the *night of the long knives, evil walks* as a *night prowler,* because a lot of attacks happened then," but the best part is that the town rocks and rolls all day long, *so for those about to rock, we salute you.* A *fly on the wall* would be insane to stay once the *high voltage* sound of the *rock 'n' roll singer* begins because she will *shake your foundations* and *rock your heart* out. If you have a *rock n roll dream,* then you could easily *R.I.P. (rock in peace)* here.

6

Everyone visiting or living around the town would be advised to *ride on the rock n roll train* at least once for the amazing experience. The trip lasts about two hours and if anyone here is interested in taking the trip, then see me and I will make all the arrangements. They say that if a *problem child* went for a *ride on* the train, then they would end upcoming back as a *rocker*.

Hells bells if you were not a *rocker* beforehand, because by the time you get off the *rock n roll train* that has let you *rock your heart* out while *rocking all the way* around town, you will say *"That's the way I wanna rock 'n' roll."* It's an expression that is used and it means that the train travels to different clubs just about every night.

The citizens of the town all agree that *rock and roll ain't noise pollution* and they say *"That's the way I wanna rock 'n' roll* and you *shook me all night long* because the music made me feel like I was being *thunderstruck; like the way T.N.T.* explodes."

There's gonna be some rockin' tonight down at *The Razor's Edge* Club because some people from the *show business* world are coming into town to listen to the *rock 'n' roll singer* and to watch their *rocker shake a leg*.

There is another club situated in a different part of town called *Satellite Blues* that was opened up by the escapees. The *Satellite Blues* Club is strictly an adults club, where patrons say *"This house is on fire* because the *soul stripper* leaves me *spellbound* by her act, especially if she does her *Sink the Pink* routine."

The special drink that is served there is a *Shot of Love* that would make any male *rocker* become a *love hungry man*. Although *she likes rock n roll*, the *soul stripper* will bring you to *meltdown* after she lets her *love bomb* explode and you get a *love at first feel* while she is singing a bluesy *love song*.

Moneytalks in this town and if it talks loud enough, you could get a *mistress for Christmas* or a *little lover*.

Many people say "You know it *ain't no fun waiting round to be a millionaire* so we will have to find another way of making money and enough of it to talk for me."

A *mistress for Christmas* is like a child's nanny who looks after children during school holidays and weekends.

7

"So what do you do for money honey?" some of the visitors would ask the people with the *stiff upper lip* (The society crowd) as they sit *back in black* limousines. The visitors rarely got an answer.

A sign in town says *"LET'S GET IT UP* AND *LET THERE BE ROCK."*

I don't know what the sign means or who it was meant for, as I have never been able to find out. I have asked many people; however they didn't know either even though they had grown up in the town.

I did hear a story from an elderly gentleman that in his childhood a *squealer* was saved from certain death after he had said to one of the escapees *"If you want blood, you've got it. I've got you by the balls* and *I put the finger on you* because I have notified the authorities to the whereabouts of you *jailbreak* escapees and they are on their way."

The Furor of the fight that followed was like *T.N.T.* going off. The Police Officials were *back in black,* and as they burst in on the escapees they shouted *"Give it up.* You've been *caught with your pants down. We've got you by the balls* now, so *if you dare* to, go ahead and try to *fire your guns* and you will be *shot down in flames.* We will not *shoot to thrill* but shoot to kill.

You say that *moneytalks,* well, here is your *down payment blues* for where you are going to. We're taking you *back in black* vans up the *Highway to Hell;* back to jail and if you think that's hell, then *hell ain't a bad place to be;* for you'll be there for at least the next twenty five years."

The informant was able to get away unharmed but he disappeared from this town not long after the recapture of the escapees and nobody knows what happened to him or if he is still alive, or where he moved to."

THE NEXT TOWN

As we were waiting to get on the bus, a few of the tourists who had taken the train trip commented on how good it was and what an amazing experience it had been. They all agreed that they liked the music that was classed rock and roll and some had even suggested that the music could be classed in many different genres.

Back on board the bus everyone said they felt relieved to be leaving the town and asked about the next town and if we would be stopping there at all.

"The next place south on the *Highway to Hell* is Belgium that is five hours from here; however there is a road side diner, about half way, where we will stop for some morning tea and yes, we will be stopping in Belgium for lunch but let me warn you now; there is always *bedlam in Belgium.*

The town is a mixture of *Sin City* and Classic Rock, so *for those about to rock, we salute you.*

On the *Sin City* side of town, which is the nice side of town, there is another woman known as *D.T.* who is so much like Rosie, a *whole lotta Rosie.* She also comes from a large Southern black family so *she's got balls* and there's no *beating around the bush* when it comes to dealing with her and she doesn't tolerate *dirty deeds done dirt cheap.*

In fact, the *riff raff* will avoid her place because they know that *she's got balls* and she will *walk all over you.* If you stick around, you will be *shot down in flames* if you try to tangle with her.

One day, someone asked D.T. *"What do you do for money honey?"*

She replied "I used to be in *show business.* At one stage I was a *soul stripper* who danced a different way to the *Bad Boy Boogie,* but I always wanted to be a *rocker* 'cos you *can't stop rock 'n' roll.*

I thought that I was *safe in New York City.* I was, until a very large strong man they called *The Jack* came into the club that I was working in, one *stormy May Day.* He gave me a drink called a *Snake Eye* followed by a *Shot of Love.*

9

All sorts of things *snowballed* from then on. I became his *little lover* until he turned into a *cold hearted man* who used to *carry me home* over his shoulder when I refused to go home with him.

The Jack grew up from being a *problem child, playing with girls* to a person who was as *hard as a rock*. He would say "*Have a drink on me* but you'll have to *come and get it.*" and when you went to get it, he would *cover you in oil* and laugh at how messy you looked. He really was *all screwed up*.

He also enjoyed putting people down in any way he could and when he had succeeded in bringing you down to your lowest level, he would make fun of you and turn nasty towards you, then he would ignore you for most of the time or just dump you, leaving you with nothing but the clothes on your back.

I told him one day that I was leaving and all he said at the time was "*Baby please don't go*, I'm *up to my neck in you* and I'll change."

He did change for a while but he was soon *back in black* and started his *Dirty Deeds Done Dirt Cheap* business. He was *back in business* not long after he had said "It *ain't no fun waiting round to be a millionaire* and *it's a long way to the top* in this *dog eat dog* world."

He charged a lot of money to do the work but his tradesmen were shoddy workers and when the customers complained about the work he would tell them that they got the work done what they wanted done and not to bother him again or he would make sure that they wouldn't bother him again.

I thought to myself "*You ain't got a hold on me.*" so I left New York City and came here, where I bought this club from the *money made* from my years of working as a *soul stripper*. *Moneytalks* but I have enough money that it shouts not talks.

My money, the purchase of my club and my old fashioned ways, started the *bedlam in Belgium* and now I have said *goodbye and good riddance to bad luck*."

The other side of Belgium, the Classic Rock side, the not so nice side; is the *dog eat dog* part of town, where *anything goes*. *The Jack* (not the one that DT knew) is known as *Big Jack* over there and is *back in black*.

10

His *Dirty Deeds Done Dirt Cheap* business has grown so much that he has had to franchise parts of it out. The franchisees are *back in black* and red uniforms unless it is something really dirty, then they will wear overalls. The tradesmen do a reasonable job but the customers still have to pay an exceedingly excessive amount of money to get the job done. Sometimes the tradesmen themselves, whilst looking at what has to be done; makes the job worse so as to force the customers to get the work done by them immediately.

There is a lot of *riff raff* on that side of town that has *guns for hire,* but will not *shoot to thrill* but to wound or kill you if you are *in the line of fire.* They will *shake your foundations* by exploding a *touch too much* of *T.N.T* near your house or they will use some *ruff stuff* on you and you might be knocked down and *kicked in the teeth* if you dare to cross them.

Some of them even work for Big Jack, carrying out his different kinds of Dirty Deeds, like if you want a husband or wife or lover off your back, then he will arrange to get the job down.

Yes, *evil walks* here but the best thing about the whole town is the attitude that you *can't stop rock 'n' roll* because *rock and roll ain't noise pollution* and *rock 'n' roll damnation* is a way of life. So *for those about to rock,* the citizens will let the *flick of the switch* to send *high voltage* music your way.

There is also an adult's only club here, where the *soul stripper* will leave you *spellbound* after performing her *"Sink the Pink,"* routine (I think that you know what I mean, just by the way I said it) and singing you a love song. Because the *girls got rhythm,* and after a *touch to much* of *whiskey on the rocks,* you would be wondering *what's next to the moon.* She is one person who you would never ask *"What do you do for money honey?"* but say instead "I'm *up to my neck in you."*

There is also a rock and roll train that travels between both sides of Belgium and *hells bells* if you were not a *rocker* beforehand, because by the time you get off the *rock n roll train* that has let you *rock your heart out* while rocking all the way around town, you will say *"That's the way I wanna rock 'n' roll."* It's an expression that is used and it means that the train travels to different clubs just about every night or in Big Jack's case going to the clubs that he has an interest in.

In this part of town, some folks would say "People are weird because *some sin for nuthin'* and end up living their lives on *the razor's edge,*

11

especially when someone like D.T, who is like a *whole lotta Rosie,* lives nearby in the good part of town."

There's the Diner up ahead that we're pulling into for a short break. Please don't wander off as we won't be here for very long.

When they pulled into the driveway of the diner, they saw a sign stating that the diner would be closed for the next week.

They stayed in Bedlam for a few hours and once back on the bus Jo said "Well, *are you ready* to say *goodbye and good riddance to bad luck* and this town? After you have *givin' the dog a bone,* we will go down the *Highway to Hell* a bit further and away from all the *bedlam in Belgium.*

Jo said "Don't worry, there's a truck stop further up the road that is sure to be open."

IN BETWEEN

Back on the road, everyone in the bus was either sleeping, reading books or magazines or they were looking out the windows. Jo had traveled this road many times and was not surprised to see that a couple of farm house had been abandoned, a few had become bigger and were growing some sort of crop besides running heads of cattle or sheep or in one case having all three; crops, cattle and sheep. She also noticed that a few places on a hill side that were once above ground mining areas, were now left as half empty craters for Mother Nature to deal with.

As the passengers began to stir Jo said "You could be *thunderstruck* and think that *that's the way I wanna rock 'n' roll* after leaving Belgium, but remember that the *Highway to Hell* is a long road and you still have a long way to go before you reach the other end. You're not even half way yet and there is still a lot to see, visit and hear about.

Still travelling south, you will pass the *bonfire of the Vanities,* more miners saying "*Let there be rock.*" as they use either the *Ballbreaker,* a *Whole Lotta Rosie* with her *big ball* or the miners in a different area saying "*Let there be rock,* please *let there be rock* and plenty of it." as they set up the equipment of *The Jack,* with its *high voltage* current, to blow up the ground that is as *hard as a rock* with *T.N.T.* If you do see them, just think that they may be in *danger* of getting hit by a piece of flying rock or other types of debris if they are not careful.

Look, there's a truck pulling out of the truck stop loaded with another *Whole Lotta Rosie* machine, *T.N.T* and look; *shes got balls* loaded on with her. This truck stop is called *Badlands* so we will stop here for our break.

You could meet many truckers who are *back in black* trucks, uniforms or just plain clothes. You may see parked trucks carrying goods like another *Whole Lotta Rosie* machine, a *big ball* or *T.N.T.* to the mines, a *big gun* that could be an old *war machine,* music *for those about to rock, high voltage* cables used for many things, *ride on* mowers, clothes or just food either in refrigerated containers or stacked on pallets.

No matter what the trucks are transporting, you can bet that they will be travelling up or down the *Highway to Hell.*

Have you noticed that all the trucks carrying *T.N.T.* are covered and a have dangerous goods sign fixed to the back tail gate?

13

I haven't mentioned yet where Hell is, have I? Well, you will see some really big billboards further down the road that will explain it, anyway *Hell ain't a bad place to be* in the end and I know that you will enjoy it there."

They stopped for half an hour, then once back on the bus Jo said "OK, now that you are refreshed and comfortable *are you ready* to continue the journey?

Oh, don't worry about the truck that's parked next to the bus and carrying *T.N.T.* as you're not in any *danger* because the detonators haven't been connected yet, so don't go having a *nervous shakedown.*

The countryside will be a bit boring for a while so we will turn on the radio and tune it into the *rocker* station. The volume, well, *let's get it up* 'cos you've already been told that *rock and roll ain't noise pollution* and that *rock 'n' roll damnation* is a way of life.

You're not even *safe in New York City* because you *can't stop rock 'n' roll* from spreading. It's like someone did *inject the venom* of rock and roll into your veins and once it took hold of you, you became a *rocker.* You became a *live wire* and it would have been like *kissin' dynamite* when it took a hold of you.

Hey, *can I sit next to you girl* until we reach the next place that we will stop at because I have found that when it comes to rock and roll most *girls got rhythm.*

Hang on! What's that I see in the distance, could it be a travelling carnival that has stopped and set up for business?

Yes, I think it is. *Baby, please don't go* getting too excited; let's make it to the carnival first. Every year about this time, the carnival camps down at the crossroads for about ten days so that all the surrounding towns can attend; that is all except one, *Decibel* who refuse to attend.

The townsfolk of Decibel believe that the surrounding towns have been damned through rock and roll. Many years ago some of their young people left and studied at the University in New Hampshire and when they returned home, they were made unwelcome because they brought rock and roll music back with them that the preacher said was the Devil's music.

14

The young people either had to go back to the way they used to live and get rid of their rock and roll music or they had to leave the town. Most of them left anyway to find work and now none of the young people are allowed to go away to college or university unless their parents or at least one of their parents go with them to make sure that they don't get caught up in the modern day music scene.

For those about to rock into the town, let me warn you, that if the citizens there find out you like rock and roll music, they would soon *cover you in oil* and leave you *burnin' alive*. Where we believe that *rock and roll ain't noise pollution,* they believe it is and that *rock 'n' roll damnation* is just that, damnation.

They say that they have never had a *problem child* because they would never let there be rock music in the town. They would even *blow up your video* to keep it out. *School days* must be boring for the kids who live there but the weekends must be worse.

What would life be without rock and roll and the *Bad Boy Boogie?*

Well, we aren't going there so let's go and have some fun at the carnival. That is if you want to stop?"

One of the passengers called out "*Who made who* think that we shouldn't stop at the carnival? You can never have a *touch too much* of fun. I haven't been to a carnival in years so it would be fun going back into my youth again, even if it is only for a few hours."

That comment made everyone laugh.

A FUN DAY

The carnival is huge and rowdy. This is a place where no-one could say "It *ain't no fun waiting around to be a millionaire*" because fun was all it was.

Jo said "As you walk through the entrance, there is a sign that reads "*ARE YOU READY* FOR FUN AND THRILLS".

Some carnies were *back in black* but for most, it was colored clothing. It is definitely a place where you *can't stand still* for too long.

The first side show attraction you come to is called *Ballbreaker*. This machine looks like a mini *Whole Lotta Rosie* and works in a similar fashion. Breaking rocks in a pattern is the idea of it and whoever gets the pattern right in an allotted amount of time wins a prize.

For the Rough Nuts who enjoy coming here, there are many shooting galleries. There is one where you have to *fire your guns* at a moving bell and if you hit it, the bell will peal out "*Hells Bells,* you got me." and after a certain amount of hits, the gun person receives the choice of a prize.

There is a paint ball area where, for safety reasons, if you are over a certain age, you can go in. There are *guns for hire* and you can *shoot to thrill* yourself especially if you shoot and hit an opponent with a paint ball. Many people have been *shot down in flames* as they are covered in paint when they come out and they are all laughing about it and saying "*Who made who* the messiest with the paint."

Don't worry; the owners make sure that there are plenty of covering garments and a clean-up area for each person who enters. No-one has ever had to enjoy the rest of their day with paint on their bodies or clothes.

There is another area called *Jailbreak,* where characters are hiding and will pop out from their cover intermittently and you will have to shoot them with one of the *guns for hire*. If you hit and knock down any of the twelve escapees, they would be sent *back on the chain gang* and you would win a prize; however, if you sent the whole twelve back in an allotted time, you could win an extra prize. The background music for that game is *Bad Boy Boogie*.

There is a *Cyberspace* challenge game where credits can be won, depending on how many flies are shot off the wall with a *high voltage* ray stick and are caught *deep in the hole,* a few inches in front of the wall. I would hate to be a real *fly on the wall* in this game.

There is a *Boogie Man* train that you ride on as it takes you through dimly lit tunnels. Some men are *back in black,* all black, as they act as a *night prowler* jumping out to frighten you by touching your arm, or the *cold hearted man* who pretends to try to *cover you in oil* but you will pass him just in the *nick of time* and he will miss hitting you with the liquid.

It is usually a scary ride so if a female is alone when she gets on the ride, another male attendant will ask *"Can I sit next to you girl,* just for your protection?"

Hells Bells is a strictly adult's only ride. It is a bell shaped cage that people are strapped into and it begins to ring and sway slowly at first, and then it builds up speed for about a minute before it starts to slow down to a stop. Even though it will only last for a few minutes, it is enough for the people when they get off to feel *thunderstruck* because of the noise and the *brain shake* that they have just received.

The shaker is another strictly adult's only ride. The riders are strapped to the walls of a cage and with the *flick of the switch* the floor shakes as if two sticks of *T.N.T.* have been detonated under your feet. The feeling for quite a while afterwards is as if *you shook me all night long.* You don't have to *hold me* back from going on that ride.

On all adult rides and games if you are caught *breaking the rules,* you will be asked to leave that particular area and are restricted from going on other rides. I don't know how the carnies police that rule, but they do. I only know of one time when a person was actually escorted from the carnival for misbehaving too much.

Getting closer to the children's attractions of games and rides, you can hear a spruiker shouting *"She's got balls;* let's see if she can *sink the pink* duck to win a prize. Yes, she wins another prize. Have the *girls got rhythm* for this game?" Children usually walk away with some sort of prize.

An unusual child's game they have is *Fling Thing.* A child will stand up on a wide platform and with the *flick of the switch* will send a medium sized disc hurtling towards a *fly on the wall,* which there are many, and if

17

the fly is moved or knocked off the wall, a prize is given to the child. It seems a very popular game with the children.

Mothers will often be heard saying to their children "Come on now, we have other things to look at, we can come back later." or "*Baby, please don't go* wandering away from me or you'll get lost."

The Good Ship is another young children's ride. The children will *ride on* a small ship that will go around a small mountain and under a small bridge that has toys sitting on it. It is built in a large but not too deep swimming pool. There are also extra attendants at this ride for the added safety of the children in case something goes wrong and for the parent's peace of mind.

Food, food and more food is everywhere and spruikers are advertising their wares. You can hear "*Come and get it*. Get your hotdogs here." or "Get your coffee here. Come and *get it hot*." Then, there is the Burger Man shouting "Burgers cooked fresh so *come and get it, get it hot* right now."

A little boy walked up to a small girl eating at one of the tables and said "*Can I sit next to you girl* 'cos I want to watch that *dog eat dog*. I just dropped my hotdog on the ground and that dog is now eating it and mommy is getting me another one."

The young children watched a man *givin' the dog a bone* before leading it away on a leash.

The little girl then turned to her mother and said "Look mommy; that lady has a *whole lot of rosie* in a big basket."

The mother replied "I think you mean roses, darling, not rosie."

When the evening comes around, an announcement is made over the loud speakers that are situated all over the carnival "*For those about to rock,* we'll be at the soundstage at seven o'clock. This is a *go zone* for any *rocker* who thinks that *rock and roll ain't noise pollution* and that *rock 'n' roll damnation* is just a way of life. We will meet you there and *let there be rock.*"

Once you've arrived there, the D.J. says "*For those about to rock, we salute you* and go and *have a drink on me* because you will become a *heatseeker* from all the dancing that you'll be doing.

Just hand in the orange ticket that you were given as you came through the gates to receive your free drink.

Look at her, the *girls got rhythm* and she sure can move to the *Bad Boy Boogie*. I bet tomorrow she will be saying "*You shook me all night long.* Well; that's what it felt like."

Back down at the *Cyberspace* pavilion, the guys are *back in black* and *spoilin' for a fight*. They line up to challenge each other by shouting "*This means war.*"

The idea is that all competitors stand on a wooden plank called *The Razor's Edge,* opposite each other and they try to hit each other by firing missiles across the room. The space between the planks is made to look like a small lagoon with a few floating obstacles that the opponent can momentarily seek cover from.

If you want blood, you don't really get it because with the special *guns for hire* and with a *flick of the switch,* instead of a trigger, they will fire a *high voltage, heatseeker* missile towards you and explode on impact with a small thud sound. A live wire will light up a *T.N.T.* sign on the jacket when they are hit in certain places. The jacket is very long and specially designed so no-one can get injured and all competitors have to wear helmets, goggles and face guards as well.

The Furor between the boys who *shoot to thrill* and those who are *shot down in flames* is very rarely *snowballed* outside, when the game is over.

The *girls got rhythm* for rock and roll and the guys have *gone shootin'* but after the guys have finished their game, they will re-joined the girls shouting "*Let there be rock* now and *let's make it shake your foundations. Are you ready,* then, let's go."

Rock and roll can be like a *love bomb* and can make you fall in *love at first feel* of the beat. Girls beware, for it can make your *little lover* a *love hungry man* for rock and roll. So *let's get it up* and start rockin'. Guys beware; the band *What's Next To The Moon* can be a *shot of love* for your little lady and may cause her to say tomorrow "*You shook me all night long.*" Don't forget if you are a heatseeker then you can have a drink on me.

When the carnival is closing for the night, would you like to stay the night at the motel down the road or would you like to keep travelling?"

19

HALFWAY

The following morning over breakfast Jo said "Wasn't the carnival a great day and a good break from all the travelling down the *Highway to Hell?*

It's good that we stopped at this motel down on the borderline of the two counties of Black Hills and *Hells Bells* for the night. Everyone should be nice and rested for the continuation of our tour.

As we continue travelling south on the *Highway to Hell,* you'll learn more about *Hells Bells* so *are you ready* to get on the road again?"

The group talked amongst themselves and agreed that the previous day had been really great as it allowed them a good break from all the sitting and sight-seeing that they had done.

Once back on the bus Jo continued "You will see loads of billboards along the road from now on but soon you will be *back in black, Black Ice* territory. *Baby, please don't go* thinking that *evil walks* in this county even though *money talks* and there are similarities with *Sin City* and Classic Rock here.

The first billboard will say "VISIT OUR WAR MUSEUM. TURN RIGHT AT THE NEXT CROSSROADS 10 MILES AHEAD". That is a very interesting place to visit so you might just want to take a detour and go there. Let me know if you would like to visit the Museum.

You would; well, that's great so let me tell you a little about the place before we get there.

At the entrance, there is a *big gun,* a *war machine* that was used during World War I, when the *first blood* of our soldiers was shed. During the *Night of the Long Knives* campaign, many soldiers with their *guns for hire* from the army found that *it's a long way to the top* of a hill when the enemy who were *back in black* uniforms was firing down at them with their *guns for hire.*

The Commanders of the big *war machine* techniques used code names to try and baffle the enemy into where they were going to strike next. One such hill with the code name *Hail Caesar,* was difficult to get a foot hold on but *come hell or high water* that's what our boys did and saying every inch of the way up *"If you want blood, you've got it."*

Eventually they took the hill and when they finally reached the top, they said to the enemy prisoners that they had just captured "I feel *thunderstruck* because *you shook me all night long* with the shells you fired from your cannons. *It's a long way to the top* and it was as *hard as a rock* getting here, but we did it."

Hail Caesar was just the first hill that had to be taken along *The Razor's Back* mountain range that they had to cross.

There is also another *big gun* on the opposite side of the entrance and this one is a *war machine* from World War II. During that war, many of the enemies were *back in black* uniforms as it made them harder to see, especially at night when they became a *night prowler*.

During that conflict the *Hail Caesar* code name was used again and many of the men fighting believed that they were on *borrowed time*. The commanders told them "You *can't stand still* because you'll become an easy target to be shot at and so will your mates. *If you want blood,* then shoot to kill not *shoot to thrill* and let the blood be from your enemy and not yours or your mates."

The soldiers also carried *guns for hire* from the army and every now and then when a soldier had temporarily ran out of ammunition he would say to the guy next to him "*Gimme a bullet,* quick *gimme a bullet.*" which he was usually given. At one stage when supplies were held up due to the truck convoys being attacked, orders came through to the soldiers to only fire your guns if you could get a good shot at the enemy.

The Air force has not been forgotten at the museum because in a hanger close by, there is the plane that spilt the *first blood* during the air conflict. The pilots would *chase the ace* of their enemy, who they nick named the *Boogie Man.* He was a *cold hearted man* because after our pilot had been *shot down in flames* and had bailed out, the *Boogie Man* would not *shoot to thrill* but shoot to kill him while he was still parachuting down to the ground.

One day in the *chase the ace* battle, one of our pilots got the *Boogie Man* in his sights and said "*If you want blood, you've got it.*" and fired hitting the cockpit, setting it alight and killing the pilot and sending the plane spiraling down in a spin.

The pilot who had fired the final shot said "Now, *fire your guns.* Your *evil walks,* no, flies, no more in these skies.

You have been *shot down in flames* and I have to watch you go down *burnin' alive*. Usually, I *shoot to thrill* but in this case it was to kill because many of our pilots have been *shot down in flames* by you. You've been flying on *the razor's edge* for too long."

After a few hours at the Museum Jo said "Don't you think it's time we continue our journey down the *Highway to Hell* to the small city of Black Ice."

Everyone got back on the bus and Jo continued "To the east and just before you reach the outskirts of the town; you can see the mining sites where a *Whole Lotta Rosie* and *The Jack* are used. This mining site has another destructive device called The *Squealer* and is operated by remote control.

The miners stand up the *T.N.T.* that has a *live wire* attached to the top of each stick, in slotted racks. The racks are then placed somewhere on or in the rock to be demolished and as a *high voltage, heatseeker* signal is sent from the remote control by a *flick of the switch,* a squealing sound is heard.

Nobody will stick around when they know that the miners are using the *Squealer* because it can cause you to feel like you have been *thunderstruck* and it will definitely *shake your foundations*. The vibrations will make you scream and shout "*You shook me all night long*."

The road is a safe distance from the mining so we won't get hit by any debris; however we are still liable to feel the vibration of the explosion slightly."

The group knew that the town was now coming into view because a billboard said "*FOR THOSE ABOUT TO ROCK* WE WELCOME YOU".

SIMILARITIES

"WELCOME TO BLACK ICE *FOR THOSE ABOUT TO ROCK*." is the sign that greets you as you actually enter the edge of the small city.

The driver turned on the microphone and Jo began "The similarities here to *Sin City, back in Black* Hills territory are the mining projects with a *Whole Lotta Rosie* and *The Jack* but here they also have The Squealer.

Moneytalks around here by the way of *Bonny* who owns several businesses and no-one has to ask her *"What do you do for money honey?"*

Her first business, which is her main money maker, is *Dirty Deeds Done Dirt Cheap* by *the Jack* of all trades. The tradesmen or women go to people's places and mow lawns, clean drains, clean windows or do small land clearing and landscaping jobs. The females often do some domestic work like cooking, cleaning, washing and ironing.

Her second business, which is becoming quite popular is, Have A *Mistress For Christmas*. A *Mistress for Christmas* is not what you are thinking; it's a novel way of advertising nannies and babysitters. Bonny employs both males and females who on *school days* will pick up and look after your child /children; however, they are specialists and will only look after one *problem child* at a time especially if that child is a *live wire*.

On the weekends, if the mother has had to go down the *Highway to Hell* to *Hells Bells* City and the father has *gone shootin'* with his mates and their *guns for hire,* the nannies will stay over at the house and look after the child /children and they have even been seen *givin' the dog a bone.*

The female nannies find that it is easier *playing with girls* because if they find that the *girls got rhythm,* they can dress them up as a *rocker* and get them to sing songs like the *Bad Boy Boogie* or *Baby, Please Don't Go.*

Boys, on the other hand can be a real *live wire* and can be a *Ballbreaker* especially if they kick it too hard. Some will go to their rooms, change and come *back in black* with their *Jailbreak* or *Fling Thing* game. Both are very boring for a female so that is where a male nanny comes in handy.

23

Bonny also owns and runs the *Satellite Blues* Club. This club is situated up on the side of a hill that has a good view of the city below. No-one seems to mind that *it's a long way to the top if you wanna to rock 'n' roll* or do the *Bad Boy Boogie.*

As you enter the club, you will be greeted and given a ticket by the doorman who will say "*Have a drink on me* during the night."

Although *she's got balls,* if there is any trouble at the club, Bonny will *send for the man* who will sort it out.

If asked, the patrons would say the same thing here that you've heard in all of the other towns, "*This house is on fire* but *Rock and roll ain't noise pollution* and *rock 'n' roll damnation* is a way of life."

Now, on the Classic Rock similarities; the main man is known as *The Jack* of the Cartel who can be a *cold hearted man* and as *hard as a rock.*

One of his businesses is also called *Dirty Deeds Done Dirt Cheap* but only on a *C.O.D.* basis and usually has his employees *back in black* and red uniforms or just plain black depending on their jobs. They are not as professional as Bonny's business and they will do a little roughing up to an unsatisfied customer or someone who wants revenge on someone else.

The Jack, who was once in *show business,* runs a shady club called *Two's Up* that plays *high voltage* music. He will say "*That's the way I wanna rock 'n' roll* 'cos my way of life is not *rock 'n' roll damnation,* anyway, *rock and roll ain't noise pollution.* Ask any *rocker* if you don't believe me."

In this part of the city, you would most probably stumble across a *problem child* who is *all screwed up* and looking for trouble, or an ex-con who was *kicked in the teeth* while attempting a jailbreak or even a *love hungry man* who will ask an unescorted female "*Can I sit next to you girl* and will you *let me put my love into you* for a couple of hours?"

Those are a couple of similarities; however, there is another small group of people who live here.

They are the upper class, the society people who walk around with a *stiff upper lip* and entertain some of the people who are high up in the *show business* or corporate world.

Mind you *moneytalks* with the society people and they regularly employ a *Mistress For Christmas* to look after a spoilt *problem child* while they go out entertaining their guests.

These society people tell their guests "Being *safe in New York City* is a lot different than being safe here, even though there is less *riff raff* here to worry about. There are fewer people wandering the streets and the law enforcement officers patrol the area quite frequently. They got here in the *nick of time* and stopped a burglar from breaking in a while ago."

The society people will never frequent the *Two's Up* Club, but occasionally have been seen at the *Satellite Blues* Club. These society people with the *stiff upper lip* must think *rock and roll ain't noise pollution* or *rock 'n' roll damnation* isn't a way of life or they wouldn't frequent the *Satellite Blues* Club.

Maybe rock and roll takes them back to their *school days* when they would say to their parents "*You ain't got a hold on me.*"

They would then go out and *shake a leg* and shout out "*Let there be rock,*" without having to worry about what other people would think of them or what their parents would say.

Have you ever wondered *who made who* rich? *It's a long way to the top* of the corporate ladder and some people will *walk all over you* just to get there.

We will have a few hours break here and we will meet at the *Thunderstruck* Café before deciding if we should continue on or stay the night and have some refreshments while we digest all that you have experienced so far."

REFLECTION

A small group of the passengers talked to Jo about something unsavory that they had witnessed that made them want to continue on straight away and immediately boarded the bus.

Jo replied to them and the rest of the tour group "In a way I am glad that you decided to continue on and reflect back whilst we are still heading south especially after what you had seen and heard.

On your trip down the *Highway to Hell,* so far, *Sin City,* way *back in Black* Hills County was where mining was the main source of employment, and the place where the Rough Nuts would say *"Let there be rock."* It was where you first learnt about a *Whole Lotta Rosie,* the *Ballbreaker* and *The Jack* that uses a *high voltage* current sent through a *live wire* to blow up the *T.N.T.* that could leave you *thunderstruck* after the explosion. Then the townies would be heard saying *"You shook me all night long."* It was the first town where *dirty deeds done dirt cheap* was not allowed and where the *jailbreak* escapees, who thought that *hell ain't a bad place to be,* were caught and taken back to jail.

The next town visited on the *Highway to Hell* was Classic Rock where *dirty deeds done dirt cheap* was prolific and a *problem child* was a normal child. Yes, that was the town that was taken over by escapees many, many years ago and told that they were given the *down payment blues* and that *hell ain't a bad place to be* as they were taken back to jail for another twenty five years. The town where *if you want blood, you've got it* because they would shoot to kill not *shoot to thrill.*

The best thing about that town was that it was a good place *for those about to rock* to be and where the citizens agreed that *rock and roll ain't noise pollution* and *rock 'n' roll damnation* was just a way of life. They would say *"You shook me all night long* with the *high voltage* music that left me feeling *thunderstruck."*

Belgium was the next town on the *Highway to Hell* that you visited. D.T. lived in this town and was the woman who was a lot like Rosie, a *whole lotta Rosie.* She was the woman who didn't tolerate *dirty deeds done dirt cheap.*

She was the woman when asked *"What do you do for money honey?"* told the story of how she came to the town and settled there after finding out that she wasn't *safe in New York City.*

26

D.T. soon found out that *moneytalks* and bought the club so she could *let there be rock* especially *for those about to rock.*

Then there was the other side of town where it was a *dog eat dog* world. *The Jack* lived there (not the one that DT knew) and was *back in business* with his *Dirty Deeds Done Dirt Cheap* and his club. *The Jack's* club was the adult's only club but they *let there be rock* there, as well as the stripper who danced the *Bad Boy Boogie* a different way.

This was the part of town, that had some *riff raff* who, if you upset them would shoot to kill and not *shoot to thrill* or you could *be kicked in the teeth* after being knocked down. That was also the town where *some sin for nuthin'* and lived on *the razor's edge* especially when D.T. who was someone like a *whole lotta Rosie* lived nearby.

Remember that after *givin' the dog a bone* and you had said *goodbye and good riddance to bad luck* and Bedlam, you continued your journey down the *Highway to Hell* before stopping at the truck stop, Badlands. The truck stop where you saw the truckers who were mainly *back in black* uniforms and their trucks that were laden with cargo like the *Whole Lotta Rosie* machine, *The Jack* equipment and *T.N.T.* for the mines, the *high voltage* cable and the *ride on* mowers.

You left the truck stop after a short break and continued south, passing the turn off to Decibel where they regarded everyone in the surrounding towns *damned* because of rock and roll. The elderly townsfolk believed that they didn't have a *problem child* anywhere in the town because they never *let there be rock* music in their town.

The carnival was the next stop and boy oh boy did you have a good time there. The side show attractions like the *Ballbreaker* that looked like a mini *Whole Lotta Rosie* machine, the shooting galleries where you were able to *shoot to thrill* everyone around when you hit the bell and it pealed out "*Hells Bells,* you got me." The Paint Ball area, where the people who had been inside came out laughing and cover in paint because they had been *shot down in flames.*

The Jailbreak area that played the *Bad Boy Boogie* music in the background and the *Cyberspace Arcade* where if a *fly on the wall* was shot off with a *high voltage* ray stick and went into the hole, you could win credits.

27

The rides for adults, where in the Boogie Man Train, the men were *back in black,* all black, would scare you by trying to throw liquid over you but you passed them just in the *nick of time* for them to miss hitting you, and the Shaker, where, when you got off you said "It felt like *you shook me all night long."* And what about the *Hells Bells* ride that left you feeling like you had been *thunderstruck* after the brain shake that you had just received.

Did you just ask *"Who made who* go on the rides?" Well, it certainly wasn't me who made you; you made your own decisions.

The children's section was equally as good as they had their own rides like The Good Ship. They had the fun game called *Fling Thing* where they had to either move or knock off a *fly on the wall* to win a prize.

Then, there were the mothers who would say to their children "*Baby, please don't go* wandering off or you'll get lost."

Oh, and don't forget that little boy who asked the girl "*Can I sit next to you girl* so I can watch that *dog eat dog."* before its owner lead it away from the crowd.

To me, the best part of the carnival was the evening when they announced "*Let there be rock* and *for those about to rock, we salute you."* Because the *girls got rhythm,* they headed for the sound stage while the guys had *gone shootin'* down at the Cyberspace Pavilion.

The guys would shoot at each other with a *high voltage, heatseeker* missile, whilst wearing specially designed clothing and head wear for safety and incorporated in the long jacket was a *live wire* that would light up a *T.N.T.* sign if it were hit in a certain place. After their game, the guys would re-join the girls for a night of rock and roll.

The following day, just outside Black Ice, you visited the War Museum. You learnt that most of the enemy was *back in black* uniforms and didn't *shoot to thrill* but shoot to kill and about the code name *Hail Caesar* that was used during both World Wars.

You saw the plane that drew first blood in the air conflict and learnt about the pilot who *shot down in flames* the enemies ace pilot who would never be *back in black.* We never did actually find out *who made who* go to war first.

28

So far, that's what you've experienced; however, better places and times are just ahead, so *let's shake a leg* and *don't hold me back* 'cos *come hell or high water* a good time is going to be had by everybody.

You will find that *hell ain't a bad place to be,* so watch for the billboards ahead to find out more.

CHOICES

A young male traveler said to his wife "This really was a good idea for our first anniversary celebration and I'm glad that we're back on the road again, and travelling the final leg of the journey to the city of *Hells Bells* at the other end of the *Highway to Hell*. Oh look, here is the first of many billboards coming up.

The billboard reads "*HELL AIN'T A BAD PLACE TO BE. HELLS BELLS* SHOWGROUNDS. TURN RIGHT INTO *BALLBREAKER* ROAD FROM THE *HIGHWAY TO HELL*. 10 MILES AHEAD
THE NEXT CARNIVAL WILL BE JULY 2ND TO 9TH. SEE YOU THERE AND COME AND *HAVE A DRINK ON ME*."

His wife replied "Well, isn't that a shame, the show was on last month but don't worry there is still plenty of things for you to do and see. What's this, another sign for the showground?"

"*THERE'S GONNA BE SOME ROCKIN'* HERE ON SEPTEMBER 15TH. COME AND HEAR THE BANDS *THUNDERSTRUCK* AND *THE RAZOR'S EDGE*."

The driver said loudly "After seeing them you'll be saying "*You shook me all night long*." I wonder if the society people, you know the ones with the *stiff upper lip*, will allow their teenagers to attend this concert."

Another billboard is coming up and what does this one say.

"*HELL AIN'T A BAD PLACE TO BE* ESPECIALLY AT THE *HELLS BELLS* CAMPING GROUND. TURN LEFT INTO *HEATSEEKER* ROAD AND FOLLOW THE SIGNS. *DIRTY DEEDS DONE DIRT CHEAP* ON A *C.O.D.* BASIS BY QUALIFIED TRADES PERSONS IF YOU NEED SOMETHING SMALL DONE".

A blond haired lady said "My friend Gabby told me about this place.
She told me that the camping ground has overnight cabins and trailers and can be rented weekly or monthly if you want to stay longer. There are powered sites for your own trailer and a section where tents can be erected. All amenities are clean and well maintained.

Near the Office and Diner are two swimming pools; one is for the younger children, and a playground. Children must be supervised at all times. Anyone caught *breaking the rules* will be asked to leave.

30

Once a fortnight the band *Who Made Who* play in the area near the swimming pools. *Who made Who* is a local band but two of the band members do shift work every fortnight at the mountain retreat."

"That's right honey." said her husband "Col told me about their trip down here."

They passed another billboard that read "*HELL AIN'T A BAD PLACE TO BE* IF YOU STAY AT THE *HELLS BELLS* MOUNTAIN RETREAT. TURN RIGHT INTO *BALLBREAKER* ROAD AND FOLLOW THE SIGNS PAST THE SHOWGROUNDS".

Then he continued saying "He also told me that this is a really peaceful and serene place to stay. Jo, please correct me if I am wrong but he also told me that the owners of the mountain retreat have built a club on the mountain that overlooks the city of *Hells Bells*. Some say that *it's a long way to the top if you wanna rock and roll* but *for those about to rock,* a short ride from the retreat in a cab is worth it.

I think he said that *Hail Caesar* cabs is the name of one of the companies run by *Dirty Deeds Done Dirt Cheap* and when you arrive at your destination, the cab driver gives you a voucher that says "*Have a drink on me* and thank you for travelling with *Hail Caesar.*"

Once at the club, if you dare to say "*Let there be rock,*" the *rising power* of the *high voltage* music will give you an *overdose* of rock and roll. If the *girls got rhythm,* you will find that she *can't stand still* and at the end of the evening will say "*You shook me all night long.*"

He looked at his wife and with a grin said "Honey, that's what you'll be saying to me if I took you up there." and then he continued "The retreat would be a good place to send a *problem child* who is *all screwed up* and is as *hard as a rock* with a *meanstreak,* just like our neighbor's grandson.

The *program start* is with a game of the mini version of a *Whole Lotta Rosie* because it helps release some of the aggression built up in the child. If you let a child *walk all over you* then they think that they've *got you by the balls,* become a *live wire* and will think *this means war* if you try to stop them.

If you *send for the man,* the child will be taken to a secluded building that is full of arcade games where they are made to play for hours but they never win.

31

The special games were made to frustrate the child and to teach them that they can't always win and get their own way.

The child can continually *shoot to thrill* their egos, with *guns for hire* in another game but will always become *thunderstruck* after being continually *shot down in flames*. Eventually, they will figure out that *if you want blood, you've got it* but it's their blood they get and a *nervous shakedown*.

Don't worry, no *evil walks* here and nobody is *damned* but a child can be like *dynamite in the machine* unless a *meltdown* process can be found safely for them to use, to start them *moving on up* to a time where they can say *goodbye and good riddance to bad luck*.

That's enough about the child, who needs a problem child anyway."

Jo said "You're absolutely right about the Retreat for both parents and problem children.

And now a bit of *back seat confidential* here. Girls, I've heard many rumors about a good looking male they call Earth Angel David, who approaches some women and says *"Can I sit next to you girl* and will you *let me put my love into you;* my love of rock and roll that is?" and then he gives them a short kiss. Oh; he doesn't do anything wrong or causes any harm, except it's said that kissing him is like *kissing dynamite*. He seems to *inject the venom* of rock and roll into your heart that makes you feel like you were *born to be wild.* Then he just disappears.

We have just seen three of the five billboards on the *Highway to Hell* and now here comes the fourth."

"HELL AIN'T A BAD PLACE TO BE IF YOU SPEND IT BY THE OCEAN. *HELLS BELLS* SEA RESORT IS THE PLACE TO BE. *DIRTY DEEDS DONE DIRT CHEAP.* ARRANGEMENTS MADE THROUGH THEIR OFFICE".

"They say that at the sea resort, they give a *global warning* for the *heatseeker* to get the beach staff to *cover you in oil;* their special oil, before you sun bake. So don't get *caught with your pants down* or you might just get sun burnt.

Baby, please don't go and be a *fly on the wall. Let's make it* to the beach concert where you will find that rock and roll will be *love at first feel* of the rhythm.

Do you want to say *"You shook me all night long?"* Well, *for those about to rock,* let the bands *Thunderstruck* and *Skies On Fire* entertain you at the Sound Shell on the main beach each Friday and Saturday night. *Rock and roll ain't noise pollution* and *rock 'n' roll damnation* is something we don't worry about, so grab your *little lover* and if *shes got rhythm,* get to the *go zone* and *let there be rock* also *have a drink on me."*

The last billboard, *"HELL AIN'T A BAD PLACE TO BE.* WELCOME TO *HELLS BELLS* CITY. *ANYTHING GOES* HERE AND *DIRTY DEEDS DONE DIRT CHEAP* ANYTIME. THE *HELLS BELLS* HOTEL IS THE PLACE TO STAY IF YOU DON'T WANT THOSE *DOWN PAYMENT BLUES."*

A more matured female asked Jo more about the sign and what there was to do in the city.

Jo replied "You want to know a little more about the *Hells Bells* City and the hotel?

Well, it's a grand hotel that enjoys having anybody staying with them, not just those with the *stiff upper lip.* (You know who I mean.) Besides they don't ask *"What do you do for money honey?"*

Above the entrance hangs a sign *"HELL AIN'T A BAD PLACE TO BE."* and in the foyer, they have some Historic City Site pictures on the wall at the *back in black* frames, including one of the *landslide* that happened fifty years ago.

Beside the service desk, where you are greeted and signed in, there is an information stand that holds many brochures about places to see and visit and up and coming events.

Once signed in, you will be escorted to your suite where you will find your luggage waiting and that the beds are not *hard as a rock.* There is room service if you wish to use it; however, there is a Dining Room that serves well-presented and reasonably priced meals.

The *big ball*-room on the top floor has been redecorated and named the *Satellite Blues* Room because *there's gonna be some rockin'* going on up there every night. The regular bands playing up there are *Dog Eat Dog* and Powerage and occasionally *Thunderstruck* will play there. They often used to play the blues up there.

33

For those about to rock who think that *it's a long way to the top to rock'n'roll,* let me tell you *this house is on fire* or rather this room is on fire and you will be *thunderstruck* when they *let it rock.* They will *shake your foundations* when the *rising power* of the *high voltage* music and the *rock 'n' roll singer* will *rock your heart out.* After a night out up there, you will be saying in the morning "*You shook me all night long.*"

The music's volume does not affect the peace and quiet of the rooms on the lower levels.

About the town; there are various shopping centers and markets, cinema complexes, parks and gardens and a casino, just to name a few places. You can *ride on The Honey Roll* Monorail to the casino if you wish. The casino has an Entertainment room called the *House of Jazz* where the jazz band *Dirty Eyes* used to play. Now, like everywhere else they *let there be rock* instead.

I personally like it there. You have to either *hold me back* or *rock me baby* otherwise I *overdose* on a *touch too much* of rock and roll and you have to *carry me home.* Most days I wish that I could be *forever young* and *R.I.P. (rock in peace.)*

Sorry about that. Now, *are you ready* to make your choice as to where you would like to go?"

DECISIONS

"Well, now you know something about *Hells Bells* City and the surrounding area and attractions at the other end of the *Highway to Hell.* As you have noticed, there aren't any *Whole Lotta Rosie* machines, *The Jack* equipment, The Squealer or *T.N.T.* anywhere to be found near here. No, this is not a mining town but a fun city and surrounding locations.

If you want blood, well, you're in the wrong place. Everybody who lives here knows that it *ain't no fun waiting round to be a millionaire.*

Money talks for those with the *stiff upper lip* and who sit *back in black* limousines and think that they are as safe here as they would be *safe in New York City.* Really, they live on *the razor's edge* and would be *thunderstruck* if some *live wire* criminal executed a well-planned smash and grab on their homes.

Baby, please don't go thinking that because you don't sit *back in black* limousines with a *stiff upper lip* that your money talks any less than theirs. Money talks for everyone, so when someone asks you *"What do you do for money honey?"* be proud of what you do and tell them."

Jo looked at the young couple and said "So, you and your *little lover* have decided to stay at the hotel for a few days. You're going to take a ride on *The Honey Roll* Monorail over to the casino and *shake a leg* in the House of Jazz and have a *whiskey on the rocks.* May I suggest that you also go to the park for a while on the weekend as they have a few activities happening there?

A more matured man is often found sitting under a tree on his big chair telling the visitors *the story of Back in Black.* You may even be *thunderstruck* when he has finished telling the story.

Listen for the spruikers calling out *"She's got balls.* Let's see if she can *sink the pink* duck." or *"Shoot to thrill* and *sink the pink* target to win a prize." or *Get it hot,* get your coffee here." or *"Get it hot,* get your hotdogs here."

A band called *Meltdown* plays down by the lagoon for a couple of hours in the afternoon. They are the sort of band that won't leave you *thunderstruck* after listening to them or have you saying *"You shook me all night long."*

Be careful that you don't become a *heatseeker* and get a *touch too much* sun as it will ruin your day if that happens. So make sure you *have a drink on me* before it does.

In the evening, you may want to go up the *Satellite Blues* Room where they *let there be rock*. Some people say that *it's a long way to the top if you wanna rock'n'roll* but *for those about to rock, this house is on fire* or should I say the room is on fire when the music starts. The following morning you'll both be saying "Wow, *you shook me all night long* but *who made who* dance all night."

Jo looked at the blonde haired woman and her husband and said "Did you say that you intend to spend a couple of days at the hotel and then go to the sea resort for a few days as well?

So, you have finally got the *shot of love* for rock and roll and now it will *walk all over you. Who made who* stand up and say *"That's the way I wanna rock 'n' roll." I put the finger on you* because you *let me put my love into you;* my love of rock and roll.

Before you head back home, back up the *Highway to Hell* in your *wheels* to New York City, are you also going to spend a few days at the mountain resort? Don't forget *it's a long way to the top if you wanna rock'n'roll* but it worth the trip up. Keep your eyes open as you might see David wandering around up there. At least he won't have to ask you to *"Let me put my love into you;* my love of rock and roll that is because it is already there."

The more matured couple told Jo that they had phoned their son and daughter and told them that they were going to be staying longer because *Hell ain't a bad place to be* and there were so many more places in the area that they wanted to visit and so much more that they wanted to do.

"No, *Hell ain't a bad place to be* and *for those about to rock, we salute you.* Remember, you *let me put my love into you;* my love of rock and roll, so don't *give it up* and *live* like there's no tomorrow and always *let there be rock.*

If those people with their *stiff upper lip* who think that they are *safe in New York City* want to *walk all over you, stand up* and say "I'm *up to my neck in you* trying to put me down.

I'm a *rocker* now and *there's gonna be some rockin'* here for *this house is on fire*. With my love of rock and roll music you will be saying to me in the mornings "*You shook me all night long.*"

Always believe that *rock 'n' roll damnation* is just a way of life and that *rock and roll ain't noise pollution*.

Now, go and have an enjoyable holiday and a safe trip home. You are welcome to come back any time you want to."

REFERENCE

BACKRACKS

Stick Around Lyrics
Love Song Lyrics
Fling Thing Lyrics
R.I.P. (Rock in Peace) Lyrics
Carry Me Home Lyrics
Crabsody in Blue Lyrics
Cold Hearted Man Lyrics
Snake Eye Lyrics
Borrowed Time Lyrics
Down on the Borderline Lyrics
Big Gun Lyrics
Cyberspace Lyrics
Dirty Deeds Done Dirt Cheap (Live) Lyrics
Dog Eat Dog (Live) Lyrics
Live Wire (Live) Lyrics
Shot Down in Flames (Live) Lyrics
Back in Black (Live) Lyrics
T.N.T. (Live) Lyrics
Let There Be Rock (Live) Lyrics
Guns for Hire (Live) Lyrics
Rock and Roll Ain't Noise Pollution (Live) Lyrics
This House Is on Fire (Live) Lyrics
You Shook Me All Night Long (Live) Lyrics
Jailbreak (Live) Lyrics
Highway to Hell (Live) Lyrics
For Those About to Rock (We Salute You) (Live) Lyrics
Safe in New York City (Live) Lyrics
Big Gun (DVD) Lyrics
Hard as a Rock (DVD) Lyrics
Hail Caesar (DVD) Lyrics
Cover You in Oil (DVD) Lyrics
Stiff Upper Lip (DVD) Lyrics
Satellite Blues (DVD) Lyrics
Safe in New York City (DVD) Lyrics
Rock N Roll Train (DVD) Lyrics
Anything Goes (DVD) Lyrics
Jailbreak (DVD) Lyrics
It's a Long Way to the Top (If You Wanna Rock 'N' Roll) (DVD) Lyrics
Highway to Hell (DVD) Lyrics

You Shook Me All Night Long (DVD) Lyrics
Guns for Hire (DVD) dirty Deeds Done Dirt Cheap (DVD) Lyrics
Highway to Hell (DVD) Lyrics

NO BULL: THE DIRECTOR'S CUT
Cover You In Oil Lyrics
Down Payment Blues Lyrics
Program Start Lyrics
Back In Black Lyrics
Shot Down In Flames Lyrics
Thunderstruck Lyrics
Girls Got Rhythm Lyrics
Hard As a Rock Lyrics
Hells Bells Lyrics
Ballbreaker Lyrics
Whole Lotta Rosie Lyrics
Let There Be Rock Lyrics
For Those About To Rock (We Salute You) Lyrics
Credits Lyrics
Shoot To Thrill Lyrics
Hail Caesar Lyrics
Rock and Roll Ain't Noise Pollution Lyrics
You Shook Me All Night Long Lyrics

IRON MAN 2
Shoot To Thrill Lyrics
Rock "N" Roll Damnation Lyrics
Guns For Hire Lyrics
Cold Hearted Man Lyrics
Back In Black Lyrics
Thunderstruck Lyrics
If You Want Blood (You've Got It) Lyrics
Evil Walks Lyrics
T.N.T. Lyrics
Hell Ain't a Bad Place To Be Lyrics
Have a Drink On Me Lyrics
The Razors Edge Lyrics
Let There Be Rock Lyrics
War Machine Lyrics
Highway To Hell Lyrics

CLIPPED
Thunderstruck Lyrics
Moneytalks Lyrics
Are You Ready Lyrics
Heatseeker Lyrics
That's the Way I Wanna Rock & Roll Lyrics

IRON MAN 2 (DELUXE EDITION) (CD/DVD)
Shoot to Thrill Lyrics
Rock "N" Roll Damnation Lyrics
Guns for Hire Lyrics
Cold Hearted Man Lyrics
Back in Black Lyrics
Thunderstruck Lyrics
If You Want Blood (You've Got It) Lyrics
Evil Walks Lyrics
T.N.T. Lyrics
Hell Ain't a Bad Place to Be Lyrics
Have a Drink on Me Lyrics
The Razors Edge Lyrics
Let There Be Rock Lyrics
War Machine Lyrics
Highway to Hell Lyrics
Shoot to Thrill (Iron Man 2 Video) Lyrics
The Making of "Shoot to Thrill" Music Video Lyrics (not used in story)
Highway to Hell (Live at River Plate Stadium, Buenos Aires, 2009 (Live)
Lyrics
Rock "N" Roll Damnation (Live at Apollo Theatre, Glasgow, 1978 (Live)
Lyrics
If You Want Blood (You've Got It) (highway to Hell Promo Clip, 1979)
Lyrics
Back in Black (Live at Plaza De Toros De Las Ventas, Madrid, 1996)
(Live) Lyrics
Guns for Hire (Live at Joe Louis Arena, Detroit, Mi, 1983) (Live) Lyrics
Thunderstruck (Live at Donington Park, 1991) (Live) Lyrics
Let There Be Rock (Live at Plaza De Toros De Las Ventas, Madrid,
1996) Lyrics
Hell Ain't a Bad Place to Be (Live at Circus Krone, Munich, 2003) (Live)
Lyrics

LET THERE BE ROCK
Go Down Lyrics
Dog Eat Dog Lyrics
Let There Be Rock Lyrics
Bad Boy Boogie Lyrics
Problem Child Lyrics
Overdose Lyrics
Hell Ain't a Bad Place to Be Lyrics
Whole Lotta Rosie Lyrics

'74 JAILBREAK
Jailbreak Lyrics
You Ain't Got a Hold on Me Lyrics
Show Business Lyrics
Soul Stripper Lyrics
Baby Please Don't Go Lyrics

BLOW UP YOUR VIDEO
Heatseeker Lyrics
That's the Way I Wanna Rock & Roll Lyrics
Mean Streak Lyrics
Go Zone Lyrics
Kissin' Dynamite Lyrics
Nick of Time Lyrics
Some Sin for Nuthin' Lyrics
Ruff Stuff Lyrics
Two's Up Lyrics
This Means War Lyrics

T.N.T
It's a Long Way to the Top (If You Wanna Rock & Roll) Lyrics
Rock & Roll Singer Lyrics
The Jack Lyrics
Live Wire Lyrics
T.N.T Lyrics
Rocker Lyrics
Can I Sit Next to You Girl Lyrics
High Voltage Lyrics
School Days Lyrics

41

SATELLITE BLUES
Satellite Blues Lyrics
Let There Be Rock (Live-Plaza de Toros, Madrid) Lyrics

WHO MADE WHO
Who Made Who Lyrics
You Shook Me All Night Long Lyrics
D.T. Lyrics
Sink the Pink Lyrics
Ride On Lyrics
Hells Bells Lyrics
Shake Your Foundations Lyrics
Chase the Ace Lyrics
For Those About to Rock (We Salute You) Lyrics

FLICK OF THE SWITCH
Rising Power Lyrics
This House Is on Fire Lyrics
Flick of the Switch Lyrics
Nervous Shakedown Lyrics
Landslide Lyrics
Guns for Hire Lyrics
Deep in the Hole Lyrics
Bedlam in Belgium Lyrics
Badlands Lyrics
Brain Shake Lyrics

FOR THOSE ABOUT TO ROCK (WE SALUTE YOU)
For Those About to Rock (We Salute You) Lyrics
I Put the Finger on You Lyrics
Let's Get It Up Lyrics
Inject the Venom Lyrics
Snowballed Lyrics
Evil Walks Lyrics
C.O.D. Lyrics
Breaking the Rules Lyrics
Night of the Long Knives Lyrics
Spellbound Lyrics

HIGHWAY TO HELL
Highway to Hell Lyrics
Girls Got Rhythm Lyrics

Walk All Over You Lyrics
Touch Too Much Lyrics
Beating Around the Bush Lyrics
Shot Down in Flames Lyrics
Get It Hot Lyrics
If You Want Blood (You've Got It) Lyrics
Love Hungry Man Lyrics
Night Prowler Lyrics

POWERAGE
Rock 'n' Roll Damnation Lyrics
Down Payment Blues Lyrics
Gimme a Bullet Lyrics
Riff Raff Lyrics
Sin City Lyrics
What's Next To The Moon Lyrics
Gone Shootin' Lyrics
Up to My Neck in You Lyrics
Kicked in the Teeth Lyrics

HIGH VOLTAGE AUSTRALIA 1975
Baby, Please Don't Go Lyrics
She's Got Balls Lyrics
Little Lover Lyrics
Stick Around Lyrics
Soul Stripper Lyrics
You Ain't Got a Hold on Me Lyrics
Love Song Lyrics
Show Business Lyrics

DIRTY DEEDS DONE DIRT CHEAP AUSTRALIAN
Dirty Deeds Done Dirt Cheap Lyrics
Ain't No Fun (Waiting 'Round to Be a Millionaire) Lyrics
There's Gonna Be Some Rockin' Lyrics
Problem Child Lyrics
Squealer Lyrics
Big Balls Lyrics
R.I.P (Rock in Peace) Lyrics
Ride On Lyrics
Jailbreak Lyrics

DIRTY DEEDS DONE DIRT CHEAP
Dirty Deeds Done Dirt Cheap Lyrics
Love at First Feel Lyrics
Big Balls Lyrics
Rocker Lyrics
Problem Child Lyrics
There's Gonna Be Some Rockin' Lyrics
Ain't No Fun (Waiting 'Round to Be a Millionaire) Lyrics
Ride On Lyrics
Squealer Lyrics

FLY ON THE WALL
Fly on the Wall Lyrics
Shake Your Foundations Lyrics
First Blood Lyrics
Danger Lyrics
Sink the Pink Lyrics
Playing with Girls Lyrics
Stand Up Lyrics
Hell or High Water Lyrics
Back in Business Lyrics
Send for the Man Lyrics

IF YOU WANT BLOOD (YOU'VE GOT IT)
Riff Raff Lyrics
Hell Ain't a Bad Place to Be Lyrics
Bad Boy Boogie Lyrics
The Jack Lyrics
Problem Child Lyrics
Whole Lotta Rosie Lyrics
Rock 'N' Roll Damnation Lyrics
High Voltage Lyrics
Let There Be Rock Lyrics
Rocker Lyrics

LIVE (SPECIAL COLLECTOR'S EDITION) 2 DISCS
DISC 1
Thunderstruck Lyrics
Shoot to Thrill Lyrics
Back in Black Lyrics
Sin City Lyrics
Who Made Who Lyrics

44

Heatseeker Lyrics
Fire Your Guns Lyrics
Jailbreak Lyrics
The Jack Lyrics
The Razor's Edge Lyrics
Dirty Deeds Done Dirt Cheap Lyrics
Moneytalks Lyrics
DISC 2
Hells Bells Lyrics
Are You Ready Lyrics
That's the Way I Wanna Rock 'N' Roll Lyrics
High Voltage Lyrics
You Shook Me All Night Long Lyrics
Whole Lotta Rosie Lyrics
Let There Be Rock Lyrics
Bonny Lyrics
Highway to Hell Lyrics
T.N.T. Lyrics
For Those About to Rock (We Salute You) Lyrics

BALLBREAKER
Hard as a Rock Lyrics
Cover You in Oil Lyrics
The Furor Lyrics
Boogie Man Lyrics
The Honey Roll Lyrics
Burnin' Alive Lyrics
Hail Caesar Lyrics
Love Bomb Lyrics
Caught with Your Pants Down Lyrics
Whiskey on the Rocks Lyrics
Ballbreaker Lyrics

AC/DC LIVE
Thunderstruck Lyrics
Shoot to Thrill Lyrics
Back in Black Lyrics
Who Made Who Lyrics
Heatseeker Lyrics
The Jack Lyrics
Money Talks Lyrics
Hells Bells Lyrics

45

Dirty Deeds Done Dirt Cheap Lyrics
Whole Lotta Rosie Lyrics
You Shook Me All Night Long Lyrics
Highway to Hell Lyrics
T.N.T Lyrics
For Those About to Rock (We Salute You) Lyrics

THE RAZOR'S EDGE
Thunderstruck Lyrics
Fire Your Guns Lyrics
Moneytalks Lyrics
The Razor's Edge Lyrics
Mistress for Christmas Lyrics
Rock Your Heart Out Lyrics
Are You Ready Lyrics
Got You by the Balls Lyrics
Shot of Love Lyrics
Let's Make It Lyrics
Goodbye and Good Riddance to Bad Luck Lyrics
If You Dare Lyrics

FLY ON THE WALL VIDEO
Fly on the Wall Lyrics
Danger Lyrics
Sink the Pink Lyrics
Stand Up Lyrics
Shake Your Foundations Lyrics

STIFF UPPER LIP
Stiff Upper Lip Lyrics
Meltdown Lyrics
House of Jazz Lyrics
Hold Me Back Lyrics
Safe in New York Lyrics
Can't Stand Still Lyrics
Can't Stop Rock 'N' Roll Lyrics
Satellite Blues Lyrics
Damned Lyrics
Come and Get It Lyrics
All Screwed Up Lyrics
Give It Up Lyrics

BLACK ICE IMPORT
Rock N Roll Train Lyrics
Skies on Fire Lyrics
Big Jack Lyrics
Anything Goes Lyrics
War Machine Lyrics
Smash N Grab Lyrics
Spoilin' for a Fight Lyrics
Wheels Lyrics
Decibel Lyrics
Stormy May Day Lyrics
She likes Rock N Roll Lyrics
Money Made Lyrics
Rock N Roll Dreams Lyrics
Rocking All the Way Lyrics
Black Ice Lyrics

STIFF UPPER LIP BONUS CD
Stiff Upper Lip Lyrics
Meltdown Lyrics
House of Jazz Lyrics
Hold Me Back Lyrics
Safe in New York Lyrics
Can't Stand Still Lyrics
Can't Stop Rock 'N' Roll Lyrics
Satellite Blues Lyrics
Damned Lyrics
Come and Get It Lyrics
All Screwed Up Lyrics
Give It Up Lyrics
Cyberspace Lyrics
Back in Black (Live) Lyrics
Hard As a Rock (Live) Lyrics
Ballbreaker (Live) Lyrics
Whole Lotta Rosie (Live) Lyrics
Let There Rock (Live) Lyrics
Stiff Upper Lip Lyrics
Safe in New York Lyrics
Satellite Blues Lyrics

BACK IN BLACK (DUAL DISC)
Hells Bells Lyrics
Shoot to Thrill Lyrics
What Do You Do for Money Honey Lyrics
Givin' the Dog a Bone Lyrics
Let Me Put My Love into You Lyrics
Back in Black Lyrics
You Shook Me All Night Long Lyrics
Have a Drink on Me Lyrics
Shake a Leg Lyrics
Rock and Roll Ain't Noise Pollution Lyrics
Hells Bells (DVD) Lyrics
Shoot to Thrill (DVD) Lyrics
What Do You Do for Money Honey (DVD) Lyrics
Givin' the Dog a Bone (DVD) Lyrics
Let Me Put My Love into You (DVD) Lyrics
Back in Black (DVD) Lyrics
You Shook Me All Night Long (DVD) Lyrics
Have a Drink on Me (DVD) Lyrics
Shake a Leg (DVD) Lyrics
Rock and Roll Ain't Noise Pollution (DVD) Lyrics
The Story of Back in Black (DVD) Lyrics
Bonus Features (DVD) (*) Lyrics (not used)

DIRTY DEEDS DONE DIRT CHEAP/ THE RAZOR'S EDGE
Dirty Deeds Done Dirt Cheap Lyrics
Love at First Feel Lyrics
Big Balls Lyrics
Rocker Lyrics
Problem Child Lyrics
There's Gonna Be Some Rockin' Lyrics
Ain't No Fun (Waiting Round to Be a Millionaire Lyrics
Ride On Lyrics
Squealer Lyrics
Thunderstruck Lyrics
Fire Your Guns Lyrics
Moneytalks Lyrics
The Razor's Edge Lyrics
Mistress for Christmas Lyrics
Rock Your Heart Out Lyrics
Are You Ready? Lyrics
Got You by the Balls Lyrics

Shot of Love Lyrics
Let's Make It Lyrics
Goodbye and Good Riddance to Bad Luck Lyrics
If You Dare Lyrics

IRON MAN 2 (COLLECTOR'S EDITION) (CD/DVD)
Shoot to Thrill Lyrics
Rock 'N' Roll Damnation Lyrics
Guns for Hire Lyrics
Cold Hearted Man Lyrics
Back in Black Lyrics
Thunderstruck Lyrics
If You Want Blood (You've Got It) Lyrics
Evil Walks Lyrics
T.N.T. Lyrics
Hell Ain't a Bad Place to Be Lyrics
Have a Drink on Me Lyrics
The Razor's Edge Lyrics
Let There Be Rock Lyrics
War Machine Lyrics
Highway to Hell Lyrics
Shoot to Thrill (Iron Man 2 Video) Lyrics
The Making of "Shoot to Thrill" Music Video Lyrics (not used)
Highway to Hell (Live at River Plate Stadium, Buenos Aires, 2009) (Live) Lyrics
Rock 'N' roll Damnation (Live at Apollo Theatre, Glasgow, 1978) (Live) Lyrics
If You Want Blood (You've Got It) (Highway to Hell Promo Clip, 1979) Lyrics
Back in Black (Live at Plaza De Toros De Las Ventas, Madrid, 1996) (Live) Lyrics
Guns for Hire (Live at Joe Louis Arena, Detroit, Mi, 1983) (Live) Lyrics
Thunderstruck (Live at Donington Park, 1991) (Live) Lyrics
Let There Be Rock (Live at Plaza De Toros De Las Ventas, Madrid, 1996) Lyrics
Hell Ain't a Bad Place to Be (Live at Circus Krone, Munich, 2003) (Live) Lyrics

STIFF UPPER LIP REISSUED
Stiff Upper Lip Lyrics
Meltdown Lyrics
House of Jazz Lyrics

49

Hold Me Back Lyrics
Safe in New York City Lyrics
Can't Stand Still Lyrics
Can't Stop Rock 'N' Roll Lyrics
Satellite Blues Lyrics
Damned Lyrics
Come and Get It Lyrics
All Screwed Up Lyrics
Give It Up Lyrics

BLACK MONEY RULES IN SIN CITY
Thunderstruck Lyrics
Shoot to Thrill Lyrics
Back in Black Lyrics
Sin City Lyrics
Who Made Who Lyrics
Heatseeker Lyrics
Jailbreak Lyrics
That's the Way I Wanna Rock & Roll Lyrics
Moneytalks Lyrics
Hells Bells Lyrics
Dirty Deeds Done Dirt Cheap Lyrics
Whole Lotta Rosie Lyrics

BIG GUN
Big Gun Lyrics
Back in Black Lyrics

MAXIMUM AC/DC
Born to Be Wild Lyrics
Forever Young Lyrics
Movin' on Up Lyrics
Classic Rock Lyrics
Global Warning Lyrics
The Good Ship Lyrics
Dead Drunk Lyrics
Back in Black Lyrics
In the Line of Fire Lyrics
Dynamite in the Machine Lyrics
Back on the Chain Gang Lyrics
Bonfire of the Vanities Lyrics

50

LET THERE BE ROCK THE MOVIE – LIVE IN PARIS
Live Wire Lyrics
Shot Down in Flames Lyrics
Hell Ain't a Bad Place to Be Lyrics
Sin City Lyrics
Walk All Over You Lyrics
Bad Boy Boogie Lyrics
The Jack Lyrics
Highway to Hell Lyrics
Girls Got Rhythm Lyrics
High Voltage Lyrics
Whole Lotta Rosie Lyrics
Rocker Lyrics
T.N.T. Lyrics
Let There Be Rock Lyrics

RIDE ON, BON!
Live Wire Lyrics
She's Got Balls Lyrics
It's a Long Way to the Top (If You Wanna Rock 'n' Roll) Lyrics
Can I Sit Next to You Girl Lyrics
The Jack Lyrics
High Voltage Lyrics
Baby Please Don't Go Lyrics
Dirty Deeds Done Dirt Cheap Lyrics
Little Lovers Lyrics
Soul Stripper Lyrics
School Days Lyrics
Carry Me Home Lyrics
Live Wire Lyrics
Hell Ain't a Bad Place to Be Lyrics
Up to My Neck in You Lyrics
Kicked in the Teeth Lyrics
The Jack Lyrics
Whole Lotta Rosie Lyrics
High Voltage Lyrics
Baby Pleases Don't Go Lyrics
Problem Child Lyrics
Fling Thing Lyrics
Ride On Lyrics

NO BULL

Back in Black Lyrics
Shot Down in Flames Lyrics
Thunderstruck Lyrics
Girls Got Rhythm Lyrics
Hard as a Rock Lyrics
Shoot to Thrill Lyrics
Boogie Man Lyrics
Hail Caesar Lyrics
Hells Bells Lyrics
Dog Eat Dog Lyrics
The Jack Lyrics
Ballbreaker Lyrics
Rock & roll Ain't Noise Pollution Lyrics
Dirty Deeds Done Dirt Cheap Lyrics
You Shook Me All Night Long Lyrics
Whole Lotta Rosie Lyrics
T.N.T. Lyrics
Let There Be Rock Lyrics
Highway to Hell Lyrics
For Those About to Rock (We Salute You) Lyrics

BONFIRE

Live Wire (Live) Lyrics
Problem Child (Live) Lyrics
High Voltage (Live) Lyrics
Hell Ain't a Bad Place to Be (Live) Lyrics
Dog Eat Dog (Live) Lyrics
The Jack (Live) Lyrics
Whole Lotta Rosie (Live) Lyrics
Rocker (Live) Lyrics
Live Wire (Live) Lyrics
Shot Down in Flames (Live) Lyrics
Hell Ain't a Bad Place to Be (Live) Lyrics
Sin City (Live) Lyrics
Walk All Over You (Live) Lyrics
Bad Boy Boogie (Live) Lyrics
The Jack (Live) Lyrics
Highway to Hell (Live) Lyrics
Girls Got Rhythm (Live) Lyrics
High Voltage (Live) Lyrics
Whole Lotta Rosie (Live) Lyrics

Rocker (Live) Lyrics
T.N.T (Live) Lyrics
Let There Be Rock (Live) Lyrics
Dirty Eyes Lyrics
Touch Too Much Lyrics
If You Want Blood You Got It Lyrics
Back Seat Confidential Lyrics
Get It Hot Lyrics
Sin City (Live) Lyrics
She's Got Balls Lyrics
School Days Lyrics
It's a Long Way to the Top (If You Wanna Rock 'n' Roll) (*) Lyrics
Ride On Lyrics
Hells Bells Lyrics
Shoot to Thrill Lyrics
What Do You Do for Money Honey Lyrics
Givin' the Dog a Bone Lyrics
Let Me Put My Love into You Lyrics
Back in Black Lyrics
You Shook Me All Night Long Lyrics
Have a Drink on Me Lyrics
Shake a Leg Lyrics
Rock and Roll Ain't Noise Pollution Lyrics

COLLECTOR'S CRATE
It's a Long Way to the Top (If You Wanna Rock 'n' Roll) Lyrics
Rock 'n' Roll Singer Lyrics
The Jack Lyrics
Live Wire Lyrics
T.N.T. Lyrics
Can I Sit Next to You Girl Lyrics
Little Lover Lyrics
She's Got Balls Lyrics
High Voltage Lyrics
Highway to Hell Lyrics
Girls Got Rhythm Lyrics
Walk All Over You Lyrics
Touch Too Much Lyrics
Beating Around the Bush Lyrics
Shot Down in Flames Lyrics
Get It Hot Lyrics
If You Want Blood (You've Got It) Lyrics

53

Love Hungry Man Lyrics
Night Prowler Lyrics
Thunderstruck Lyrics
Fire Your Guns Lyrics
Moneytalks Lyrics
The Razor's Edge Lyrics
Mistress for Christmas Lyrics
Rock Your Heart Out Lyrics
Are You Ready Lyrics
Got You by the Balls Lyrics
Shot of Love Lyrics
Let's Make It Lyrics
Goodbye and Good Riddance to Bad Luck Lyrics
If You Dare Lyrics

HIGH VOLTAGE
It's a Long Way to the Top (If You Wanna Rock 'n' Roll) Lyrics
Rock 'n' Roll Singer Lyrics
The Jack Lyrics
Live Wire Lyrics
T.N.T. Lyrics
Can I Sit Next to You Girl Lyrics
Little Lover Lyrics
She's Got Balls Lyrics
High Voltage Lyrics

BOXSET – 17CD
Jailbreak
You Ain't Got a Hold on Me Lyrics
Show Business Lyrics
Soul Stripper Lyrics
Baby, Please Don't Go Lyrics
Dirty Deeds Done Dirt Cheap Lyrics
Love at First Feel Lyrics
Big Balls Lyrics
Rocker Lyrics
Problem Child Lyrics
There's Gonna Be Some Rockin' Lyrics
Ain't No Fun (Waiting Round to Be a Millionaire Lyrics
Ride On Lyrics
Squealer Lyrics
It's a Long Way to the Top (If You Wanna Rock 'n' Roll) Lyrics

Rock 'N' Roll Singer Lyrics
The Jack Lyrics
Live Wire Lyrics
T.N.T. Lyrics
Can I Sit Next to You Girl Lyrics
Little Lover Lyrics
She's Got Balls Lyrics
High Voltage Lyrics
Go Down Lyrics
Dog Eat Dog Lyrics
Let There Be Rock Lyrics
Bad Boy Boogie Lyrics
Problem Child Lyrics
Overdose Lyrics
Hell Ain't a Bad Place to Be Lyrics
Whole Lotta Rosie Lyrics
Rock 'N' Roll Damnation Lyrics
Down Payment Blues Lyrics
Gimme a Bullet Lyrics
Riff Raff Lyrics
Sin City Lyrics
What's Next to the Moon Lyrics
Gone Shootin' Lyrics
Up to My Neck in You Lyrics
Kicked in the Teeth Lyrics
Riff Raff Lyrics
Hell Ain't a Bad Place to Be Lyrics
Bad Boy Boogie Lyrics
The Jack Lyrics
Problem Child Lyrics
Whole Lotta Rosie Lyrics
Rock 'N' Roll Damnation Lyrics
High Voltage Lyrics
Let There Be Rock Lyrics
Rocker Lyrics
Highway to Hell Lyrics
Girls Got Rhythm Lyrics
Walk All Over You Lyrics
Touch Too Much Lyrics
Beating Around the Bush Lyrics
Shot Down in Flames Lyrics
Get It Hot Lyrics

55

If You Want Blood (You've Got It) Lyrics
Love Hungry Man Lyrics
Night Prowler Lyrics
Hells Bells Lyrics
Shoot to Thrill Lyrics
What Do You Do for Money Honey Lyrics
Givin' the Dog a Bone Lyrics
Let Me Put My Love into You Lyrics
Back in Black Lyrics
You Shook Me All Night Long Lyrics
Have a Drink on Me Lyrics
Shake a Leg Lyrics
Rock & roll Ain't Noise Pollution Lyrics
For Those About to Rock (We Salute You) Lyrics
I Put the Finger on You Lyrics
Let's Get It Up Lyrics
Inject the Venom Lyrics
Snowballed Lyrics
Evil Walks Lyrics
C.O.D. Lyrics
Breaking the Rules Lyrics
Night of the Long Knives Lyrics
Spellbound Lyrics
Rising Power Lyrics
This House Is on Fire Lyrics
Flick of the Switch Lyrics
Nervous Shakedown Lyrics
Landslide Lyrics
Guns for Hire Lyrics
Deep in the Hole Lyrics
Bedlam in Belgium Lyrics
Badlands Lyrics
Brain Snake Lyrics
Fly on the Wall Lyrics
Shake Your Foundations Lyrics
First Blood Lyrics
Danger Lyrics
Sink the Pink Lyrics
Playing With Girls Lyrics
Stand Up Lyrics
Hell or High Water Lyrics
Back in Business Lyrics

56

Send for the Man Lyrics
Who Made Who Lyrics
You Shook Me All Night Long Lyrics
D.T. Lyrics
Sink the Pink Lyrics
Ride On Lyrics
Hells Bells Lyrics
Shake Your Foundations Lyrics
Chase the Ace Lyrics
For Those About to Rock (We Salute You) Lyrics
Heatseeker Lyrics
That's the Way I Wanna Rock N Roll Lyrics
Meanstreak Lyrics
Go Zone Lyrics
Kissin' Dynamite Lyrics
Nick of Time Lyrics
Some Sin for Nuthin' Lyrics
Ruff Stuff Lyrics
Two's Up Lyrics
This Means War Lyrics
Thunderstruck Lyrics
Fire Your Guns Lyrics
Moneytalks Lyrics
The Razor's Edge Lyrics
Mistress for Christmas Lyrics
Rock Your Heart Out Lyrics
Are You Ready Lyrics
Got You by the Balls Lyrics
Shot of Love Lyrics
Let's Make It Lyrics
Goodbye and Good Riddance to Bad Luck Lyrics
If You Dare Lyrics
Thunderstruck Lyrics
Shoot to Thrill Lyrics
Back in Black Lyrics
Who Made Who Lyrics
Heatseeker Lyrics
The Jack Lyrics
Moneytalks Lyrics
Hells Bells Lyrics
Dirty Deeds Done Dirt Cheap Lyrics
Whole Lotta Rosie Lyrics

You Shook Me All Night Long Lyrics
Highway to Hell Lyrics
T.N.T. (Live) Lyrics
For Those About to Rock (We Salute You) (Live) Lyrics
Hard as a Rock Lyrics
Cover You in Oil Lyrics
The Furor Lyrics
Boogie Man Lyrics
The Honey Roll Lyrics
Burnin' Alive Lyrics
Hail Caesar Lyrics
Love Bomb Lyrics
Caught with Your Pants Down Lyrics
Whiskey on the Rocks Lyrics
Ballbreaker Lyrics
Stiff Upper Lip Lyrics
Meltdown Lyrics
House of Jazz Lyrics
Hold Me Back Lyrics
Safe in New York City Lyrics
Can't Stand Still Lyrics
Can't Stop Rock 'N' Roll Lyrics
Satellite Blues Lyrics
Damned Lyrics
Come and Get It Lyrics
All Screwed Up Lyrics
Give It Up Lyrics

AC/DC VINYL BOX
Live (Double) Lyrics
High Voltage Lyrics
T.N.T. Lyrics
Dirty Deeds Done Dirt Cheap Lyrics
Let There Be Rock Lyrics
Powerage Lyrics
If You Want Blood You Got It Lyrics
Highway to Hell Lyrics
Back in Black Lyrics
For Those About to Rock (We Salute You) Lyrics
Flick the Switch Lyrics
Fly on the Wall Lyrics
Who Made Who Lyrics

58

Blow Up Your Video Lyrics
The Razor's Edge Lyrics
Ball Breaker Lyrics
Stiff Upper Lip Lyrics

BACK IN BLACK
Hells Bells Lyrics
Shoot to Thrill Lyrics
What Do You Do for Money Honey Lyrics
Givin' the Dog a Bone Lyrics
Let Me Put My Love into You Lyrics
Back in Black Lyrics
You Shook Me All Night Long Lyrics
Have a Drink on Me Lyrics
Shake a Leg Lyrics
Rock and Roll Ain't Noise Pollution Lyrics

BAD BOYS IN TORINO 1984
Guns for Hire Lyrics
Back in Black Lyrics
Rock 'n' Roll Ain't Noise Pollution Lyrics
Bad Boy Boogie Lyrics
T.N.T Lyrics
The Jack Lyrics
Flick of the Switch Lyrics
Hells Bells Lyrics
Highway to Hell Lyrics
Whole Lotta Rosie Lyrics
Let There Be Rock Lyrics
For Those About to Rock (We Salute You) Lyrics

STIFF UPPER LIP EP
Stiff Upper Lip (Album Version) Lyrics
Cyberspace (Non-LP Track) Lyrics
Hard as a Rock (Live) Lyrics
Back in Black (Live) Lyrics
Whole Lotta Rosie (Live) Lyrics

LIVE U S 86 – 88
Who Made Who Lyrics
Hells Bells Lyrics
Nick of Time Lyrics
Fly on the Wall Lyrics

Shake Your Foundations Lyrics
She's Got Balls Lyrics
Whole Lotta Rosie Lyrics
Let There Be Rock Lyrics
Highway to Hell Lyrics
T.N.T. Lyrics
For Those About to Rock (We Salute You) Lyrics

THE FAMILY JEWELS
Baby, Please Don't Go (DVD) (Live) Lyrics
Show Business (DVD) Lyrics
High Voltage (Promo Clip) (Multimedia Track) Lyrics
It's a Long Way to the Top (If You Wanna Rock 'N' Roll) (Promo...)
Lyrics
T.N.T. (DVD) (Live) Lyrics
Jailbreak (DVD) Lyrics
Dirty Deeds Done Dirt Cheap (DVD) (Live) Lyrics
Dog Eat Dog (DVD) Lyrics
Let There Be Rock (DVD) Lyrics
Rock 'N' Roll Damnation (DVD) Lyrics
Sin City (DVD) Lyrics
Riff raff (DVD) Lyrics
Fling Thing/Rocker (DVD) Lyrics
Whole Lotta Rosie (DVD) Lyrics
Shot Down in Flames (DVD) Lyrics
Walk All Over You (DVD) Lyrics
Touch Too Much (DVD) Lyrics
If You Want Blood (You've Got It) (DVD) Lyrics
Girls Got Rhythm (DVD) Lyrics
Highway to Hell (DVD) Lyrics
Hells Bells (DVD) Lyrics
Back in Black (DVD) Lyrics
What Do You Do for Money Honey (DVD) Lyrics
Rock and Roll Ain't Noise Pollution (DVD) Lyrics
Let's Get It Up (DVD) Lyrics
For Those About to Rock (We Salute You) (DVD) Lyrics
Flick of the Switch (DVD) Lyrics
Nervous Shakedown (DVD) Lyrics
Fly on the Wall (DVD) Lyrics
Danger (DVD) Lyrics
Sink the Pink (DVD) Lyrics
Stand Up (DVD) Lyrics

Shake Your Foundations (DVD) Lyrics
Who Made Who (Promo Clip) (Multimedia Track) Lyrics
You Shook Me All Night Long (DVD) Lyrics
Heatseeker (Promo Clip0 (Multimedia Track) Lyrics
That's the Way I Wanna Rock N Roll (DVD) Lyrics
Thunderstruck (DVD) Lyrics
Moneytalks (DVD) Lyrics
Are You Ready (DVD) Lyrics

PLUG ME IN COLLECTOR'S EDITION 3 DVD SET
High Voltage (DVD) Lyrics
It's a Long Way to the Top (If You Wanna Rock 'n' Roll) (DVD) Lyrics
School Days (DVD) Lyrics
T.N.T. (DVD) Lyrics
Live Wire (DVD) Lyrics
Can I Sit Next to You Girl (DVD) Lyrics
Baby Please Don't Go (DVD) Lyrics
Hell Ain't a Bad Place to Be (DVD) Lyrics
Rocker (DVD) Lyrics
Rock 'n' Roll Damnation (DVD) Lyrics
Dog Eat Dog (DVD) Lyrics
Let There Be Rock (DVD) Lyrics
Problem Child (DVD) Lyrics
Sin City (DVD) Lyrics
Bad Boy Boogie (DVD) Lyrics
Highway to Hell (DVD) Lyrics
The Jack (DVD) Lyrics
Whole Lotta Rosie (DVD) Lyrics
Baby Please Don't Go (DVD) (*) Lyrics
Problem Child (DVD) Lyrics
Dirty Deeds Done Dirt Cheap (DVD) (*) Lyrics
Rock 'n' Roll Damnation (DVD) (*) Lyrics
Bonus Material (DVD) (*) Lyrics (Not Used)
Shot Down in Flames (DVD) Lyrics
What Do You Do for Money Honey (DVD) Lyrics
You Shook Me All Night Long (DVD) Lyrics
T.N.T./Let There Be Rock (DVD) Lyrics
Back in Black (DVD) Lyrics
T.N.T. (DVD) Lyrics
Shoot to Thrill (DVD) Lyrics
Guns for Hire (DVD) Lyrics
Dirty Deeds Done Dirt Cheap (DVD) Lyrics

61

Flick of the Switch (DVD) Lyrics
Bedlam in Belgium (DVD) Lyrics
Back in Black (DVD) Lyrics
Highway to Hell (DVD) Lyrics
Whole Lotta Rosie (DVD) Lyrics
For Those About to Rock (We Salute You) (DVD) Lyrics
Gone Shootin' (DVD) Lyrics
Hail Caesar (DVD) Lyrics
Ballbreaker (DVD) Lyrics
Rock and Roll Ain't Noise Pollution (DVD) Lyrics
Hard as a Rock (DVD) Lyrics
Hells Bells (DVD) Lyrics
Ride On (DVD) Lyrics
Stiff Upper Lip (DVD) Lyrics
Thunderstruck (DVD) Lyrics
If You Want Blood (You've Got It) (DVD) Lyrics
The Jack (DVD) Lyrics
You Shook Me All Night Long (DVD) Lyrics
Hells Bells (DVD) (*) Lyrics
Gone Shootin' (DVD) (*) (Take) Lyrics
Rock Me Baby (DVD) (*) Lyrics
Bonus Material (DVD) (*) Lyrics (Not Used)
She's Got Balls (DVD) Lyrics
It's a Long Way to the Top (If You Wanna Rock 'n' Roll) (DVD) Lyrics
Let There Be Rock (DVD) Lyrics
Bad Boy Boogie (DVD) Lyrics
Girls Got Rhythm (DVD) Lyrics
Guns for Hire (Band Rehearsal) Lyrics
This House Is on Fire (DVD) Lyrics
Highway to Hell (DVD) Lyrics
Girls Got Rhythm (DVD) Lyrics
Let There Be Rock (DVD) Lyrics
Guns for Hire (DVD) Lyrics
Shoot to Thrill (DVD) Lyrics
Sin City (DVD) Lyrics
This House Is on Fire (DVD) Lyrics
Back in Black (DVD) Lyrics
Bad Boy Boogie (DVD) Lyrics
Rock and Roll Ain't Noise Pollution (DVD) Lyrics
Flick of the Switch (DVD) Lyrics
Hells Bells (Multimedia Track) Lyrics
Bonus Material (DVD) (*) Lyrics (Not Used)

BACK IN BLACK/YOU SHOOK ME ALL NIGHT LONG

Back in Black Lyrics
You Shook Me All Night Long Lyrics

BIBLIOGRAPHY

Backracks: http://music.aol.com/artist/acdc/album

No Bull: The Directors Cut: http://music.aol.com/artist/acdc/album

Iron Man 2: http://music.aol.com/artist/acdc/album

Clipped: http://music.aol.com/artist/acdc/album/page10

Iron Man 2 (Deluxe Edition) (CD/DVD):
http://music.aol.com/artist/acdc/album

Let There Be Rock: http://music.aol.com/artist/acdc/album/page/12

'74 Jailbreak: http://music.aol.com/artist/acdc/album/page/12

Blow Up Your Video: http://music.aol.com/artist/acdc/album/page10

T.N.T: http://music.aol.com/artist/acdc/album/page/12

Who Made Who: http://music.aol.com/artist/acdc/album/page/11

Flick Of The Switch: http://music.aol.com/artist/acdc/album/page/11

For Those About To Rock (We Salute You):
http://music.aol.com/artist/acdc/album/page/11

Highway To Hell: http://music.aol.com/artist/acdc/album/page/11

Powerage: http://music.aol.com/artist/acdc/album/page/11

High Voltage Australia 1975:
http://music.aol.com/artist/acdc/album/page/12

Dirty Deeds Done Dirt Cheap Australia:
http://music.aol.com/artist/acdc/album/page/9

Dirty Deeds Done Dirt Cheap:
http://music.aol.com/artist/acdc/album/page/12

Fly On The Wall: http://music.aol.com/artist/acdc/album/page/11

If You Want Blood (You've Got It):
http://music.aol.com/artist/acdc/album/page/11

Live (Special Collector's Edition):
http://music.aol.com/artist/acdc/album/page/9

AC/DC Live: http://music.aol.com/artist/acdc/album/page/7

The Razor's Edge: http://music.aol.com/artist/acdc/album/page/10

Ballbreaker: http://music.aol.com/artist/acdc/album/page/8

Stiff Upper Lip: http://music.aol.com/artist/acdc/album/page/7

Black Ice Import: http://music.aol.com/artist/acdc/album/page/3

Satellite Blues: http://music.aol.com/artist/acdc/album/page/6

Stiff Upper Lip: http://music.aol.com/artist/acdc/album/page/6

Fly On The Wall Video: http://music.aol.com/artist/acdc/album/page/11

Back In Black (Dual Disc): http://music.aol.com/artist/acdc/album/page/4

Dirty Deeds Done Dirt Cheap/The Razor's Edge:
http://music.aol.com/artist/acdc/album/page/3

Iron Man 2 (Collector's Edition) (CD/DVD):
http://music.aol.com/artist/acdc/album

Stiff Upper Lip Reissued: http://music.aol.com/artist/acdc/album/page/7

Big Gun: http://music.aol.com/artist/acdc/album/page/8

Black Money Rules In Sin City:
http://music.aol.com/artist/acdc/album/page/7

Maximum AC/DC: http://music.aol.com/artist/acdc/album/page/6

Let There Be Rock The Movie – Live In Paris:
http://music.aol.com/artist/acdc/album/page/7

Ride On, Bon!: http://music.aol.com/artist/acdc/album/page/7

No Bull: http://music.aol.com/artist/acdc/album/page/8

Bonfire: http://music.aol.com/artist/acdc/album/page/7

Back In Black/You Shook Me All Night Long:
http://music.aol.com/artist/acdc/album/page/9

Collector's Crate: http://music.aol.com/artist/acdc/album/page/3

High Voltage: http://music.aol.com/artist/acdc/album/page/12

Box Set 17 CD: http://music.aol.com/artist/acdc/album/page/5

AC/DC Vinyl Box: http://music.aol.com/artist/acdc/album/page/5

Stiff Upper Lip EP: http://music.aol.com/artist/acdc/album/page/5

Back In Black: http://music.aol.com/artist/acdc/album/page/11

Bad Boys In Torino 1984: http://music.aol.com/artist/acdc/album/page/8

Live U S 86 – 88: http://music.aol.com/artist/acdc/album/page/8

The Family Jewels: http://music.aol.com/artist/acdc/album/page/4

Plug Me In: http://music.aol.com/artist/acdc/album/page/8;
jsessionid=5803D2785C130310613037

ABOUT THE AUTHOR

I was 59 years old; a mother of three very special and supportive children and a grandmother of three wonderful grandsons (I now have five grandchildren.) when I started writing my first book whilst watching a Bon Jovi concert DVD. (I am an avid fan, if you can call me that; crazy is more like it.)

I write from the heart and I really enjoyed writing the book, so I wrote another using a different artist, and the books kept coming to me and I kept writing them.(with a little help from above.)

Because I use different artist/artists song titles I have to be very careful with Copyright so a lot of legal requirements have to be taken into consideration before publishing the books. I also needed a name that would connect my books to each other; so the "Song Title Series" books began.

All my books are short stories; however it depends on how many song titles there are to be used, as to the length of the book. Some artists didn't have enough song titles on their own so I combined them with a few other artists. Other artists had that many song titles that I could have written a novel; but it would have ended up being boring.

Challenges I like, so writing books with various artists are a lot of fun and need careful thinking.

Why should I have all the fun writing the books and not be able to share them with everyone; so I have converted them into large print books so that you can share my fun as well.

Hopefully in the not too distant future; the books will also be available as audio books so that no-one will miss out on my fun and enjoyment of writing these unique books. I hope that you enjoy reading them.

My web site www.songtitleseries.com is the place to visit for updates of new books and the place to purchase other titles in all formats.

TESTIMONIALS

The song titles series are books that were intriguing and were hard to believe that these short stories were written within the incorporated song titles of the artists that are mentioned in the titles. I loved what I have read so far and think that anyone with an imagination and love of music as the author you will surely enjoy reading these.
L.K. Brisbane Australia.

Joan Maguire Books are very nice, I enjoy reading them so much, they are hard to put down!! Especially when she does one about Bonjovi and their songs!!!
If I can say, it is worth every penny, when you buy one!!! The Books make nice presents, for a person whom loves to read!!! I can guarantee that you will LOVE these books, because I do!!!!!!!!!
Dawn from Newark, Delaware in the United States of America

I am Susie and would like to tell you guys, how much I am enjoying Joan Maguire's Books!! They are very enjoyable, and they are something that you do not ever want to put down!! I really enjoy these books; I can't wait until the next one that she puts out!!!!!!! I say go to your local book store, today and get one, you will not be disappointed!!!!!
Sue-from the United States of America

After reading through your range of books I felt I must compliment you Joan on the imaginative and entertaining way in which you presented each group and the Musicians in those groups. The way the stories were constructed is a credit to your work ethic. These must have taken considerable time to piece together and it is obviously a work of love for you.
I wish you all the success you truly deserve and look forward to seeing you next time you visit Tamworth.
Peter Harkins
Managing Director Cheapa Music
Country Music Capital Tamworth

www.ingramcontent.com/pod-product-compliance
Lightning Source LLC
Chambersburg PA
CBHW060157070426
42447CB00033B/2184